D1378517

RIVERS IN WORLD HISTORY

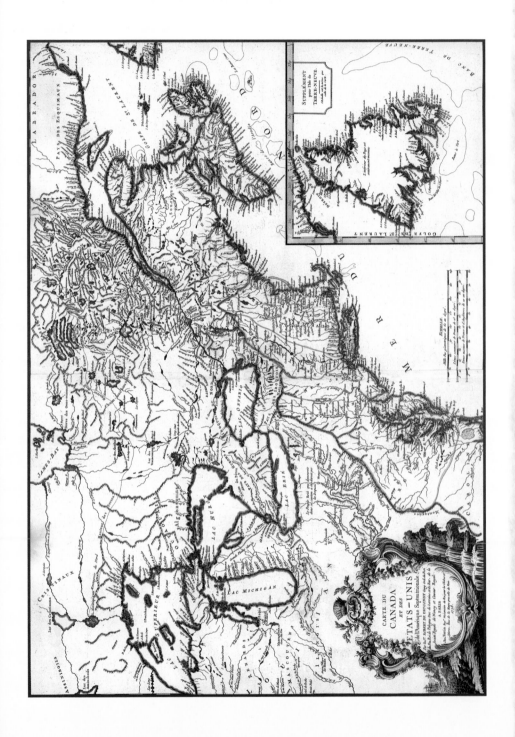

RIVERS IN WORLD HISTORY

THE ST. LAWRENCE RIVER

Tim McNeese

CHELSEA HOUSE
PUBLISHERS
A Haights Cross Communications ✕ Company ®
Philadelphia

FRONTIS: The waters of the St. Lawrence River originate from the St. Louis River, which flows into the southwestern portion of Lake Superior (upper left corner of map) and eventually into Lake Ontario. From Lake Ontario, the St. Lawrence, which is called the Kaniatarowanenneh, or "big waterway," by the Mohawks, travels 800 miles before emptying into the Gulf of St. Lawrence.

CHELSEA HOUSE PUBLISHERS

VP, NEW PRODUCT DEVELOPMENT   Sally Cheney
DIRECTOR OF PRODUCTION   Kim Shinners
CREATIVE MANAGER   Takeshi Takahashi
MANUFACTURING MANAGER   Diann Grasse

Staff for THE ST. LAWRENCE RIVER

EXECUTIVE EDITOR   Lee Marcott
EDITOR   Christian Green
PRODUCTION EDITOR   Noelle Nardone
PHOTO EDITOR   Sarah Bloom
SERIES AND COVER DESIGNER   Keith Trego
LAYOUT   21st Century Publishing and Communications, Inc.

A Haights Cross Communications ✛ Company ®

First Printing

9 8 7 6 5 4 3 2 1

Library of Congress Cataloging-in-Publication Data

McNeese, Tim.
   The St. Lawrence River / Tim McNeese.
      p. cm.—(Rivers in world history)
   Includes bibliographical references and index.
   ISBN 0-7910-8245-8 (hardcover)
   1. Saint Lawrence River—Juvenile literature. 2. Saint Lawrence River Valley—Juvenile literature. 3. Saint Lawrence River—History—Juvenile literature. 4. Saint Lawrence River Valley—History—Juvenile literature. I. Title: Saint Lawrence River. II. Title. III. Series.
F1050.M38 2005
971.4—dc22
                                                      2004022018

All links and Web addresses were checked and verified to be correct at the time of publication. Because of the dynamic nature of the Web, some addresses and links may have changed since publication and may no longer be valid.

CONTENTS

1

The River That Walks

In a northern land traversed by hundreds of icy waterways, the St. Lawrence River is considered so singularly important that it is known as the River of Canada. Centuries ago, the Native Americans who lived along its banks had their own name for the St. Lawrence: "the River that Walks." No river has played as important a role in Canada's history or provided beneficial waters to more of its people than the St. Lawrence. Indian villages once flanked its shores, and the earliest Europeans who came to the area understood its importance in the development of early New World economies such as the fur trade. Some of Canada's most historically important battles have been fought within sight of the St. Lawrence. The country's great eastern cities, including Montreal and Quebec, stand as urban sentinels above the river's banks. Today, the St. Lawrence is a mighty highway of commerce; a legacy that began when the first Native American trade canoes plied its waters. Just as every generation of the river's inhabitants has tapped the St. Lawrence for its livelihood, so modern Canadians use their great river to generate hydroelectric power. From its early indigenous peoples to today's cosmopolitan residents, the St. Lawrence has remained a vital waterway.

The St. Lawrence ranks as one of the truly significant world rivers. It is the fifteenth longest river worldwide and is third in length among Canada's watercourses, shorter than the Mackenzie River and the Yukon, which flow across western Canada. The river is not especially long—only about 800 miles or so—but it is part of one of the longest inland waterways in the world. When the St. Lawrence is included with the five Great Lakes that lie west of its course—Lakes Ontario, Erie, Huron, Michigan, and Superior—it becomes a link in a course stretching 3,000 miles, spanning more than half of the North American continent.

The St. Louis River, the origin of the St. Lawrence River, drains into the southwestern corner of Lake Superior. Water

The St. Lawrence flows past Quebec City—the second-largest city and capital of the province of Quebec, and a major trading port renowned for its textile mills, pulp and paper mills, and chemical plants.

flows from Great Lake to Great Lake, "gathering force as it races over falls and rapids on its way to the [Atlantic] Ocean."[1] Other rivers also reach the St. Lawrence, but directly, as northern tributaries, and add their flow to its course. These include the Ottawa, St. Maurice, and Saguenay Rivers (which receives its water from Lake St. John), as well as the Richelieu River, which reaches the St. Lawrence from the south. The St. Lawrence River is the recipient of a vast drainage system covering nearly 700,000 square miles, including territory in both Canada and the United States. Two million gallons of freshwater reach the St. Lawrence every second from Lake Ontario, the easternmost of the Great Lakes. This vast water flow forces the current of the St. Lawrence to remain steady and constant, requiring the delivery of 250,000 cubic feet of water to the Atlantic Ocean every second. Experts have calculated the volume as "enough water to give every man, woman, and child in America over 50 baths every day."[2]

Because the St. Lawrence receives vast amounts of lake water, its flow is extremely clean—free from silt and mud that often cloud other North American rivers. As water passes through the Great Lakes, its flow is slowed by the huge bodies of water and silt settles to the lake bottoms. In addition, as the St. Lawrence receives lake water, its flow is generally constant, maintaining the level of the river and keeping flooding to an absolute minimum. In fact, the level of the St. Lawrence River rarely varies more than 10 to 12 feet, regardless of the season. In contrast, many of the world's other major rivers are prone to annual flooding.

The banks of the modern St. Lawrence are home to millions of residents who rely on the river for drinking water, recreation, and industry and as a major inland trade highway connecting it with all five Great Lakes. Approximately one of every four Canadians, roughly 10 to 11 million people, live in the region, making the St. Lawrence Valley the most densely populated region of Canada. The two largest cities in the province of Quebec, Montreal and Quebec City, are situated along the river's northern bank. Montreal alone boasts an urban population of 3.6 million, and Quebec City is home to more than 700,000. Other prominent cities located within the St. Lawrence River valley include Ottawa (1.1 million), Hamilton (700,000), Trois-Rivières (140,000), and Saguenay (150,000).

The formation of the St. Lawrence River valley extends far back into the recesses of geologic time. According to geologists, the river's course was formed millions of years ago. A hard rock bed, known as the Canadian Shield, ran parallel to a bed of soft rock. As violent, natural upheavals such as volcanic activity and earthquakes occurred, these two segments of soft and hard rock collided with one another, causing the land surface above to drop to a lower level, creating an elongated rift. Eventually, this newly created valley line sank low enough to allow the waters of the Atlantic Ocean to flow into the region and inundate the landscape.

Although these ancient events helped create the course of the St. Lawrence, the river itself is much younger. In more recent millennia, between 13,000 and 10,000 B.P. (Before Present), this Canadian landscape was covered with a massive layer of ice more than a mile thick. As this giant ice sheet moved, it pushed the sunken soft rock layer deeper into the earth's surface. With the passage of several thousand years, violent upthrusts pushed this sunken region upward. Before the land reached an adequate elevation, however, waters again flowed in from the Atlantic Ocean, forming a vast inland sea in the region of the modern-day Great Lakes. As the geologic rock bed continued to shift and rise, the single inland body of water became several immense lakes, as well as a plethora of smaller lakes. With the rising of the inland landscape, the freshwater sea began to empty into the soft rock trough created millions of years earlier. This trough, filled with a rush of lake water, reached toward the Atlantic. The river formed by this series of geologic dominoes was the early St. Lawrence. Although the prehistoric events that created the St. Lawrence were no different than those that resulted in the creation of other significant waterways in North America—such as the Mississippi, Missouri, and Ohio Rivers—one significant difference was the direction the river flowed.

Most North American rivers flow from the north to the south; the St. Lawrence is one of the few lengthy rivers that flows from west to east. This factor sometimes causes some confusion for those viewing the St. Lawrence on a map:

> When pilots, ship captains, and geographers talk about any river, they use the terms below and above to locate spots along the river. These terms can be confusing if you are looking at a map of the St. Lawrence. The river flows from the southwest to the northeast, and on a flat map it seems as though the northeastern, or ocean, end is "above" the southwestern, or lake, end. However, this is not true. The part of any river closest to its mouth is considered to be "below" the part of the river closest to its source. It is important to remember these terms when talking or reading about a river.[3]

The St. Lawrence has been home to wildlife for tens of thousands of years; humans were a later arrival. Once they arrived and began to tap the natural resources of the great eastern Canadian river, though, the history of the St. Lawrence was forever altered.

2

Natives along the River

Today, no one is certain exactly when the first human beings reached the banks of the St. Lawrence River. Modern anthropologists continue to change the earliest date for the arrival of Native Americans in the great woodland regions of the Northeast, but 5,000 to 7,000 years ago has become the most widely accepted period of time for their arrival. Even thousands of years ago, as these first people reached the region of the St. Lawrence, they were practicing divergent arts and social customs, and developing into different culture groups.

South of the St. Lawrence and centered in modern-day New York State, the Lamoka culture hunted using projectile points that archeologists have unearthed throughout the region. Other weapons and tools that they used included "bone and antler knives, fishing hooks, awls, hide scrapers and even whistles."[4] To the east and north, another culture, identified today as the Laurentian culture (named after the St. Lawrence River), had developed. This indigenous group lived in eastern New York, New England, and north to the St. Lawrence River. These early peoples also relied on stone and bone tools and weapons. Among the artifacts unearthed at Laurentian sites are harpoons and slate spear points.

Today, Canada is home to a wide variety of Native American groups, from the Athapaskans of the western provinces to the Inuits (Eskimos) of the Maritime provinces. Two extended cultural groups, the Algonquian peoples and the Eastern Woodland Iroquoians are native to the St. Lawrence River region. These early inhabitants relied on hunting and fishing for their food; they also practiced rudimentary agriculture. By 3,000 years ago, both groups had developed various woodland cultures, living in the thick forests of the region and felling trees to erect homes and make boats for use on the local rivers, including the St. Lawrence and its tributaries. Some Native groups carved out long, heavy dugout canoes, hacked from a single, good-sized tree. Others made sleeker, swifter canoes with a wooden framework covered with large, overlapping pieces of tree bark. The Algonquians often built their canoes from birch bark, whereas the Iroquoians used elm bark.

Throughout the Northeast, Native Americans developed different tribal identities and structures during the 500 years between A.D. 1000 and the arrival of Europeans in North America. Many of these modern-day tribal groups were in place by A.D. 1250. Generally, the tribes of the Eastern Woodland peoples have been identified by their language stocks: the Algonquian and the Iroquoian. The Algonquians ranged over a larger territory than the Iroquoians. Modern anthropologists include as Algonquians those tribes east of the St. Lawrence and centered along the Atlantic Coast, such as the Micmac, Malecite, Passamaquoddy, and Eastern and Western Abenaki, as well as a variety of New England tribes, such as the Mohican, Wampanoag, Narragansett, Massachusett, and Pequot. Situated north of the St. Lawrence were the Montagnais, who lived along the Gulf of St. Lawrence; the Attikamek; Algonquin (whose tribal name is sometimes confused with the Algonquian language stock); and Nipissing tribes. Algonquian tribes living farther removed from the river region included the Cree, Sauk, Fox, and Ottawa.

When Europeans arrived along the St. Lawrence River during the late 1500s, they typically encountered Iroquoian-speaking tribes, including the St. Lawrence Iroquois, Huron, Mohawk, Oneida, and others. Although the first Europeans to reach the region of the St. Lawrence thought of the Native Americans they encountered as largely the same people, they eventually came to distinguish among the various tribes.

THE ABENAKIS

The Abenakis were among the first Native Americans to encounter Europeans in the region of the St. Lawrence. They made their homes along the major rivers of northern New England and southern Quebec during the early 1600s. Sometimes referred to as the Wabenakis, "People of the Dawn Land," the Abenakis were a group of Algonquian tribes. They were divided into the Eastern Abenakis, which included the Kennebecs and Penobscots, among others, and the Western Abenakis. During the 1600s and 1700s, an Indian alliance group called the Abenaki Confederacy was formed and included the Western and Eastern Abenakis, as well as the Malecites, Passamaquoddys, and Micmacs. The Abenakis became staunch allies of the French during the seventeenth century, partially through the efforts of an extremely successful colonizer named Samuel de Champlain. The Western Abenakis cooperated in the expansion of the French presence along the St. Lawrence during the 1600s and traded furs with the French. During the early years of the seventeenth century, the region may have been home to approximately 10,000 Eastern Abenakis and 5,000 Western Abenakis.

ABENAKI HOMES AND FAMILIES

The Abenakis lived in villages along the streams of the Northeast. Those of the east lived in dome-shaped and square houses with roofs that sloped like pyramids and were shingled with bark. The houses had a smoke hole at the top because a fire burned in the middle of the house's floor. Deerskins were used as door flaps to cover the entrance into the bark house. Western Abenakis built long houses with sloping, arching rooflines from birch bark. Several families lived alongside one another under the same roof.

Typically, the Abenaki domestic culture centered on several, interrelated families who lived together in the same lodge, which served as the tribe's basic social and economic unit. The family line was charted through the family's males. The men of each village were expected to provide their families with food through hunting, engage in warfare with neighboring tribes, and make the tools and erect the houses and lodges. The men hunted caribou, deer, and bears, and trapped beaver and a variety of other small game animals, as well as birds. They fashioned conical moose calls to lure the great shaggy beasts during a hunt. They sometimes ran down their quarry on foot.

Women did much of the agricultural work, including the annual harvesting, and prepared and cooked most of the food. They also gathered wild foods, including berries, nuts, potatoes, wild cherries, and other fruits. They sewed the clothing for themselves, their husbands, and their children. They were also entrusted with the care and raising of their young.

Villages were governed by chiefs who were recognized for their leadership abilities; sometimes the role was passed from father to son. On occasion, Eastern Abenaki chiefs were also medicine men, or shamans; after the 1600s, they were referred to as sagamores. Western Abenaki chiefs often led their village until their death, but their power of authority was relatively limited.

The Abenakis traded extensively, bartering goods with other neighboring tribes. Much of this intertribal trade was greatly reduced after the arrival of the Europeans, specifically the French, British, and Dutch. From that time on, furs were the chief item the Abenakis traded. They also fought with their neighbors. Before they joined the Abenaki Confederacy, the Micmacs repeatedly engaged the Eastern Abenakis in war; while the Western Abenakis fought the Iroquois. Before the Western Abenakis entered into a fight, men and women sat down together in a war council to discuss the pros and cons; everyone present was free to speak. If the consensus was to fight, the war chief was authorized to ask for volunteers to join him. Those who agreed painted their faces and bodies with special colors. Nearly all Indian groups relied on the same weapons of war, including the bow and arrow, knife, spear, and war club.

THE HURONS

The seventeenth-century Hurons played a crucial role during the years when New France was established along the St. Lawrence. The Hurons referred to themselves as the Wyandottes, or Wyandots, which means "islanders" or "People of the Peninsula." When European explorers first reached the St. Lawrence at the end of the 1500s, the Hurons lived in the St. Lawrence River valley. By 1600, they inhabited a region called Huronia, which included the territory between Georgian Bay (the northeastern part of Lake Huron) and Lake Ontario. At that time, the Hurons numbered 16,000 to 30,000, although their numbers dropped to about 10,000 by the mid-1600s. Many modern-day Wyandottes live in Kansas and Oklahoma, but there are about 2,700 living in the province of Quebec.

The Hurons likely originated alongside other Iroquoian speakers in the Mississippi River valley, but elements of the group had migrated north by the 1500s. The Hurons met with French explorer Jacques Cartier in 1534 and developed trade alliances with Samuel de Champlain. They fought a series of wars with the Iroquois sometime during the 1500s, perhaps earlier, and were driven out of some areas of the St. Lawrence River valley. For years after those violent intertribal encounters, the Hurons allied themselves with the Algonquians and thus against the Iroquois. They also fought alongside the French. For much of the early seventeenth century, the Hurons dominated the beaver pelt trade, serving as middlemen between the French and tribes located farther from the St. Lawrence River. Over time, through prolonged contact, the Hurons intermarried with the French.

The Hurons were led by clan civil and war chiefs. These chiefs sought counsel with their male relatives, and decisions were reached when a consensus was clear. Any decision was not binding for every individual in a village, and if decisions were made on a tribal level, they were not binding for every village. As with many other tribes in the St. Lawrence region, the Huron Confederacy was led by a council of chiefs who represented each tribe; the confederacy had no power to dictate or intervene in purely tribal matters.

VILLAGE LIFE AMONG THE HURONS

When Champlain arrived along the St. Lawrence during the early 1600s, he found the Hurons living in 18 semiautonomous villages. The villages included longhouses and public spaces. The largest villages were surrounded by a wooden wall of sharpened logs that provided security and defense. Some of the Huron villages were home to 2,000 people living in approximately 100 longhouses. Most of the villages had populations of fewer than 1,000 inhabitants. Such village sites were never permanent. After a site had been occupied for 10 to 20 years, the wooden buildings began to deteriorate, garbage and refuse became a problem, and the trees in close proximity to the village had been cut down for firewood and other purposes.

The typical Huron village house was a pole-frame, bark-covered (elm, cedar, and ash bark were most popular) domicile that measured 25 to 30 feet in width and 100 to 150 feet in length. (Some longhouses were 240 feet long!) The houses featured long barrel vaults, the curving ceilings marked with smoke holes to allow the fires inside to ventilate. A long center passage made up the main inner structure that connected the complex of rooms. Inhabitants of a longhouse, typically 8 to 24 interrelated families, slept along the sides of the house, but during winter months, people often slept on the floor near a fire for warmth. Beds were little more than woven rush mats, which were also used as flooring and for doors.

The Hurons, whom French explorer Samuel de Champlain encountered in the early 1600s, lived in villages that were composed of pole-frame, bark-covered dwellings known as longhouses. Shown here is the sleeping area, which was set up along the side of the longhouse. In the winter, the Hurons slept on the floor, close to the fire.

Such houses might be made snug in winter and airy in summer, but they were smoky, hard to keep clean, and prone to flea and mouse infestation.

Huron men and women had designated tasks. The women were the farmers, growing fields of corn, beans, squash, and sunflowers. The men often raised small patches of tobacco for ceremonial purposes. Women also gathered wild foods, including blueberries and other fruits, nuts, and even acorns when food was scarce. The women also wove mats, baskets, and nets from hemp, reeds, bark, and corn husks. They fashioned leather pouches, which they decorated with porcupine quills.

The men hunted game, including deer, bears, a variety of waterfowl, and smaller animals, using the bow and arrow. Bears might be trapped but not immediately killed. They would be kept—sometimes for a year—fattened up, and then killed for special feasts. Dogs were common in Huron camps as companions and beasts of burden, but they, too, were eaten. Along the banks of the rivers, including the St. Lawrence, Huron men fished for whitefish, catfish, pike, and other species. They also harvested clams, crabs, and turtles for consumption. The men carved wooden items, such as utensils, bowls, and shields, and made weapons and tools from stone. They also made clay pipes for smoking.

The Hurons traded extensively in the region of the St. Lawrence even before the arrival of the Europeans. Huron trade patterns were so broad that their trade routes took them to the eastern Great Lakes, as well as throughout the St. Lawrence River region. Their common trade goods included corn and tobacco, on which they sometimes held a monopoly, as well as animal pelts, dried berries, mats, fish, hemp, chert (flint-like rock), and wampum beads. The wampum beads were small, handmade from whitish mollusk shells, and strung in standard lengths. Such beads became equivalent to a form of currency. Tribes that regularly traded with the Hurons included the Petuns, who traded for tobacco, and the northern Algonquian peoples. The Nipissings were also important Huron trading partners; they traded fish and furs for Huron corn.

THE MONTAGNAIS AND NASKAPIS

As with other St. Lawrence tribes, the Montagnais were among the first to come in contact with early French explorers, and they developed intricate alliances with the new European arrivals. The name "Montagnais" is a French word that means "mountaineers." Another group who is closely related to the Montagnais is the "Naskapi," a Montagnais word that means "uncivilized people." The Montagnais called themselves "Nenenot," which translates as "the People." Today, many Naskapis and Montagnais call themselves the "Innu."

The Montagnais occupied the territory that ran from the Gulf of St. Lawrence to James Bay, along the northeastern coast of Hudson Bay to Ungava Bay, and east to the coast of the Labrador Sea. The Montagnais shared this region with other tribal groups, including the East Cree, who lived in the western region, and the Naskapis, who occupied the northlands; the Montagnais lived in the south and east. Much of this region is highly wooded, cut through by numerous waterways and streams. The land often is considered extremely remote and rugged; territory where moose lived in abundance. The Naskapi portion of the territory was less wooded: It featured more open meadowlands, where caribou roamed in large numbers. When the first Europeans arrived at the end of the fifteenth century, the Montagnais numbered approximately 4,000 and the Naskapis about 1,500. Today, their combined number hovers close to 15,000.

LIFE AMONG THE MONTAGNAIS AND NASKAPIS

Montagnais society was built on a loosely connected group of 25 to 30 small, independent hunting (or winter) bands, all interrelated by marriage. In each Montagnais band, there were several lodge groups that consisted of 15 to 20 people. A named band, or division of the tribe, would include two or three combined winter bands, perhaps as many as 300 people total. Among the Montagnais, families could pledge membership to any band they chose. Those men who served as band chiefs did not hold formal power over their people because band decisions were reached by a consensus of the band's members. In fact, the Montagnais practiced a high level of independence:

> Within the lodge groups there was no real dependence of one individual on another, since sexual relations were not limited to marriage, divorce was easy to obtain, and children were in many ways considered a group responsibility. These structures and relations encouraged a general egalitarianism.[5]

Such bands typically lived independently from one another during most of the year but several would come together during the summer alongside or at the mouths of rivers, including the St. Lawrence, for communal fishing and hunting, as well as socialization. Tribal members updated one another on who had died, become married, given birth, and a host of other family changes. Such a gathering might bring 1,000 to 2,000 people together for a shared summer.

The Montagnais and Naskapis lived in several different styles of houses. One was an expansive cone-shaped dwelling covered with birch bark that could provide shelter for up to 20 people. A fire for cooking and heat burned in the center of the dwelling, with the smoke escaping through a smoke hole at the peak of the shelter. Mats of rush or skin provided bedding and spaces for lounging. The Naskapis also built large A-frame or rectangular lodges that could accommodate several families. They used leather covering fashioned from caribou hides, which were not sewn together as a single sheath but were overlapped.

As was common among Native American groups, the Montagnais men were the hunters; their quarry included moose, caribou (for the Naskapis), bears, other four-footed animals, and a variety of waterfowl. Hunters often tried to chase down their prey, diverting them, if possible, into a river or body of water, where hunters in birch-bark canoes could make the kill. Winter hunters attempted to force the animals into deeper snows, slowing their escape. Women caught smaller game, such as porcupine, rabbits, and beaver, in snares.

Along the Labrador coast, the Montagnais and Naskapis hunted seals using bone-tipped harpoons. (The seals provided meat; their skins were fashioned into soft, water-repellant clothing; and seal oil was used to repel mosquitoes.) In winter, the men fished through the ice by cutting holes in it and lowering their lines into the icy water. Before the Montagnais were pushed north of the St. Lawrence River by neighboring tribes, they had access to a greater variety of food sources. The women kept small gardens and harvested wild foods such as berries, grapes, apples, and a variety of bulbs. The Montagnais also tapped maple trees for syrup.

Montagnais-Naskapi arts included several varieties of snowshoes and clothing styles. Caribou-skin clothing was common among the Naskapis. Robes were made from bear, moose, or beaver skins. In winter, fur pants, sewn rabbit blankets, and hooded winter coats, which were lined with animal fur, were common. Moccasins were sometimes made from sealskin. Leather or skin clothing was commonly decorated with red ocher paint and greasepaint, which was applied to clothing in a series of geometrical patterns; the Indian artisans used bone or antler painting tools to do this. Sometimes, the patterns, which included parallel lines, triangles, and leaf motifs, were stamped on the clothing.

THE IROQUOIS

For centuries, the Iroquois were the enemies of many different Algonquian-speaking tribes. The name Iroquois was used by the Algonquian speakers as a derogatory term; it has been translated as "the real adders," "the terrible people," and "the frightening people." The name used by the Iroquois was Kanonsionni, "League of the United (Extended) Households." Modern Iroquois call themselves the Haudenosaunee, "the People of the Longhouse." During the seventeenth century, perhaps as many as 20,000 Iroquois were associated with the member nations, including the Onondaga, Mohawk, Seneca, Oneida, and Cayuga tribes. Today, approximately 70,000 Iroquois Indians live in settlements and reservations in the United States and Canada.

The Iroquois peoples date to as early as A.D. 800, when they began to cultivate crops in their villages in modern-day New York State. Although the tribes spoke the same language stock, they operated largely independently and sometimes warred with each other. Sometime between 1450 and 1600, an Onondaga shaman named Hiawatha established the Iroquois League or Iroquois Confederacy, whose membership included the Five Iroquois Nations. During the early 1700s, the Tuscarora joined as the sixth. (For additional information on this Native political organization, enter "Iroquois Confederacy" into any search engine and browse the many sites listed.)

The leadership of the Iroquois League consisted of 50 hereditary chiefs, or sachems, from the member tribes. Each chiefdom was named for the original leader who held that tribal post. Although all the sachems were men, they were usually selected by the women of the tribes. The tribes were represented by two divisions within the league. Within these divisions, intertribal debates took place as part of great council and all such discussions took place within a system of "strict clan, division, and tribal protocols, in a complex system of checks and balances."[6] Member tribes maintained a significant level of latitude to pursue policies that they believed reflected their own interests, although they were loyal to the friendship among the tribes. When the Founding Fathers established the United States and its new government during the days of the American Revolution, they used the Iroquois League as a model of democratic confederation.

LIFE AMONG THE IROQUOIS

Iroquois villages were often led by a chief or headman and a council of elders, such as clan chiefs. Village chiefs might be chosen to represent tribal units as small as a single household. Together, these tribal chiefs represented their collective village, as well as the nation of the confederacy at general council sessions.

During the early 1700s, the Iroquois lived in fortified villages surrounded by palisade fences and consisting of several longhouses. These bark-covered family complexes were known by the Iroquois as the *ganonh'sees* and were erected by the men of the tribe but owned by the women. (Iroquois women enjoyed a significant amount of prestige and recognition within their tribe. They could nominate and recall clan chiefs, and they were in charge of most village activities and events, including marriages.)

Like the houses of other tribes of the Northeast, the Iroquois longhouses provided lodging for multiple families, usually 5 to 20. An average longhouse was 60 feet in length and 18 to 20 in width. The roof was arched and supported by a series of ridgepoles that ran along the length of the house. Longhouses might stand 20 feet along the center ridgeline. Walls consisted of large pieces of birch bark that measured approximately four by six feet. Where birch was scarce, the Iroquois relied on elm, ash, cedar, basswood, or hemlock. These houses had entry doors at each end and few, if any, windows or openings. This allowed the longhouses to be cool and airy in summer and kept warm air in during the winter. Beds lined the walls, and each family hung animal-skin curtains to provide some basic privacy.

Women served as agriculturalists, raising corn, beans, and squash, the three crops that collectively became known as the

Three Sisters, because of their importance as staple foods in the Indian diet. Corn was the most common staple and was used in several kinds of dishes, including soups, stews, breads, and puddings. Women also gathered wild food such as greens, nuts, seeds, roots, berries, and mushrooms. The men usually did the hunting, but some women joined them on longer hunting forays to help dry the meat. The men hunted the standard large and small animals, from moose to squirrels. By the 1700s, the Iroquois were cultivating their own orchards and raising peaches, pears, and apples.

Deerskin clothing was common among the Iroquois. The women wore leather skirts and shirts; men wore breechclouts and shirts during summer and leggings in winter. The adults wore moccasins, but children usually went barefoot. Iroquois artisans, usually women, decorated clothing with dyed porcupine quills. Other artists fashioned tools and weapons from bone, antlers, and wood. Men carved wooden masks of grotesque human faces, which were used in the curing ceremonies of the False Face Society. To provide transportation on local rivers and lakes, the Iroquois men carved elm-bark canoes sometimes 25 feet in length.

THE ARRIVAL OF THE EUROPEANS

Prior to the arrival of the Europeans, tens of thousands of Native Americans lived along the banks of the St. Lawrence River and across hundreds of square miles of woodland territory between the Great Lakes and the Atlantic Coast. Their cultures varied slightly in many ways, and there were enough differences among the dozens of tribes that even the earliest European arrivals were eventually able to make note of them. Few, if any, of these tribes kept to themselves and avoided contact with their neighbors. Indian groups often viewed one another skeptically—cautiously—regarding one another as inferiors, but there were connections, usually in the form of trade. Goods passed

This illustration from *Canadian Scenery Illustrated*, entitled "Indian Scene on the St. Laurence," depicts a group of Native Americans traveling on the river in canoes. Several tribes, including the Montagnais, East Cree, and Naskapi, lived along the river's waters.

steadily and regularly among tribes, and the benefits had to be considered mutual or war might result.

Native American tribes warred with each other constantly prior to the arrival of Europeans. Their worlds were small and territorial, and competition for access to natural resources was inevitable. They fought for hunting rights in a region or for access to a river here or a sacred ground there. The forests were often filled with wildlife, but the Indians still fought for control of those grounds because food was always a precious commodity and a tribe, village, or clan that had not prepared adequately for the harsh Canadian or New England winter might suffer greatly.

Against this backdrop of fiercely independent tribalism, competition for natural resources, repeated wars and skirmishes, and long-standing trade alliances, the vanguard of the European arrivals in the New World of the North reached the waters of the St. Lawrence River by the final decade of the fifteenth century. Once they reached the lands of these ancient residents of the St. Lawrence, life for Native Americans would never be the same.

3

The French Reach
the St. Lawrence

In 1492, a Genoan mapmaker and sea captain accidentally changed the history of the world. That autumn, Christopher Columbus, sailing on behalf of the king and queen of Spain, traveled westbound across the Atlantic Ocean with expectations of reaching the riches of the Orient. Although he set out in the right direction from Spain to reach Cathay (modern-day China) and Cipangu (modern-day Japan), he had underestimated the distance by approximately 9,000 miles. After 10 weeks of sailing, he reached the Western Hemisphere, which includes North and South America. Columbus spent the following decade exploring Caribbean waters, certain he had landed in Asia. When he died in 1506, he was still unaware that he had found a completely new landmass. Other Europeans, however, knew that Columbus had not reached the Orient but had instead found a new continent. European monarchs from England to France to Portugal were soon competing to stake their own claims in the lands that, by 1507, were referred to as America.

Within five years of Columbus' first voyage to the New World (he would sail to America on four separate voyages), the English monarch, King Henry VII, hired his own Genoese sea captain, Giovanni Caboto (John Cabot), who had immigrated to England in 1495. Given one ship, a 50-ton caravel called the *Matthew*, Cabot and a crew of only 18 seamen sailed across the North Atlantic in 1497. He first reached the modern-day Canadian province of Newfoundland, which he named as a "new found land." He returned to England, and an extremely pleased Henry dispatched Cabot back across the North Atlantic the following year, this time with four ships and 300 men. Henry's instructions to his explorer were to find a water route through the New World—the Northwest Passage, as it came to be known—so he and others who followed could reach the Orient. The passage did not exist, but Cabot and his frustrated men explored farther along the inlets and bays of Newfoundland and Labrador. Although the mission failed, Cabot returned to England a hero. He became known as the Great Admiral, and everywhere he went in London, "the English ran after him like mad people."[7] It was on Cabot's voyages that the English first laid claim to territory in the New World. (For additional information on this explorer, enter "John Cabot" into any search engine and browse the many sites listed.)

The English did little to follow up on Cabot's discoveries and explorations. France, however, did send explorers, and those voyages led to the establishment of a French empire in the New World. The first French-sponsored voyage of discovery to North America came in 1524. That year, King Francis I sent yet another Italian seafarer, Giovanni da Verrazzano, with four ships to stake a French claim and continue the search for the Northwest Passage. Storms crippled several of Verrazzano's ships on their voyage across the Atlantic; he managed to reach the shores of North America with one, the *Dauphin*, which arrived along the coast in April 1524. He searched in vain for the Northwest Passage from modern-day Newfoundland to South Carolina, but on his return to France, he informed the king that he still believed such a route existed.

Distracted by a war with Spain, Francis I waited a decade before he sent yet another explorer to North America. This man was not an Italian as the others had been but a master mariner from St.-Malo, the leading seaport of Brittany, a region situated on the English Channel that had only recently come under French control. In 1534, Jacques Cartier was 43 years old, "a stocky man with a sharply etched profile and calm eyes under a high, wide brow . . . and with a beard which bristled pugnaciously."[8] Like Columbus, Cabot, and Verrazzano before him, Cartier was an excellent shipmaster and navigator. Between 1534 and 1542, this intrepid sea captain made three voyages to the New World, following in the footsteps of those who sailed before him and exploring Newfoundland and Labrador. Cartier also sailed farther west, into the St. Lawrence River.

French explorer Jacques Cartier mistakenly believed that the St. Lawrence River, which he called La Grande Rivière, or Great River, was the Northwest Passage to the Orient. When he traveled up the St. Lawrence in 1535, he encountered rapids near what is today Montreal and discovered that the St. Lawrence was just another inland waterway.

His voyages became models of exploration, and hardship was never far away. Still, Cartier never lost a ship or even one of his crewmembers at sea.

Cartier set out on his first voyage on April 20, 1534, and reached Newfoundland in less than three weeks. His two ships, manned by 122 men, completely circumnavigated Newfoundland. That May, Cartier entered the Gulf of St. Lawrence by way of the Strait of Belle Isle, whose shore was littered with giant pieces of ice. During most of his days sailing along the Newfoundland coast, the land was shrouded in fog. Occasionally, he and some of his men landed longboats along various beaches and explored. They encountered the Micmac Indians, an Algonquian tribe who lived on Newfoundland's northern coast. The encounters between Europeans and Native Americans went well, because the Micmacs were interested in trading, an intent they signaled to Cartier by "holding up fur pelts on sticks and gesturing the French ashore."[9]

Cartier sailed on to Labrador and farther into the Gulf of St. Lawrence. Some of his crew caught sight of a polar bear and killed it, finding its meat extremely tender and tasty. There were more Natives, including the Beothuks from Newfoundland, who were out in birch-bark canoes on their annual seal hunt. As his ships passed along stretches of barren, rocky coastline, Cartier became convinced that he had reached an especially desolate country. In his journal, he noted, "I did not see a cartload of good earth. To be short I believe that this was the land that God allotted to Cain."[10] Local storms plagued his ships and made passage through choppy waters difficult. As his vessels passed into the Gulf of Lawrence, the wide mouth of the St. Lawrence River, however, "he was beginning to suspect the truth, that it was the mouth of a powerful river."[11]

As he sailed farther west into the Gulf of Lawrence, his small ships struggled against the gulf's strong current, and with each passing mile, the landscape took on a beauty of its own. His earlier views of the coast had been unimpressive, but Cartier was now passing through a land of newfound beauty. Cartier noted that one acre of this land was "worth more than all the New Land [Newfoundland]." [12] As he sailed farther into the Gulf of Lawrence, the Breton captain passed the Magdalen Islands and the north shore of modern-day Prince Edward Island. Everywhere, the land was inviting:

> It was a wonderful country. The heat of July had covered the open glades with white and red roses. There were berries and currants in abundance and a wild wheat with ears shaped like barley. The trees were of many familiar kinds, white elm, ash, willow, cedar, and yew. To the north and west were high hills, but these were vastly different from the stern mountains of Newfoundland and the barrenness of the north shore. There was friendliness in their green-covered slopes and a welcome in their approach to the water's edge. [13]

By July 2, Cartier had reached Gaspe Harbor and encountered yet another Indian tribe, a migrant tribe of Huron-Iroquois called the Laurentians. The Breton sea captain met with the tribe's chief, Donnaconna, and offered him gifts. The two men established a mutual friendship, and Donnaconna, "clothed in a black bearskin," [14] even allowed two of his sons—Taignoagny and Domagaya—to return to France with Cartier. There, they could learn the French language and in the future act as inter-preters between the French and their people. As a goodwill gesture, Cartier dressed the chief's sons "in shirts and colored coats, with red caps, putting a copper chain around each of their necks, with which they seemed much pleased." [15]

As storms in the region continued, Cartier decided to turn around and return home. He also understood that the season was getting on and did not want to get caught in icy storms without adequate provisions. As his ships turned east and sailed out of the Gulf of Lawrence, he believed that the inlet represented the Northwest Passage. He could not have known that, in fact, the St. Lawrence River lay before him and with it a great waterway into the interior of North America. Before leaving Gaspe Harbor, he and his men fashioned a 30-foot tall cross and erected it along the coast, along with a piece of wood bearing an inscription: "Vive le Roy de France" (Long live the king of France).

CARTIER RETURNS TO THE RIVER

Francis I was extremely pleased with Cartier's reports of his New World explorations, including news of a potential river passage to the Orient. He ordered a second voyage and three ships for Cartier, including a large flagship and two smaller craft, one a little galleon called a pinnance. Francis told his captain to "explore beyond les Terres Neufves" (Newfoundland and Labrador), and "to discover certain far-off countries."[16] The sons of Donnaconna studied their French and excited Cartier with information concerning the modern-day St. Lawrence River. They spoke of a large body of freshwater far to the west, a reference to Lake Ontario. They also told him that the Gulf of Lawrence was the entrance to the Great River of Hochelaga (Montreal). By May 1535, Cartier, his crew, and their ships were ready for a voyage of new explorations and discoveries.

In August, the ships passed the Bay of Seven Islands, along the Labrador coast. On August 10, the feast day of St. Lawrence, Cartier was again in the mouth of the gulf he had reached the previous year. In honor of the saint, he dubbed the gulf "La Baye Sainct Laurins." (He had not intended to call the river by the same name, but those who followed his explorations did not distinguish between the gulf and the river. Cartier always called the St. Lawrence River "La Grande Rivière," the Great River.) Soon, the French ships were headed up the river. By August 30, they passed the site of Tadoussac, at the mouth of a river that the sons of Donnaconna referred to as Saguenay. The chief's sons had regaled Cartier with stories of a mythical rich kingdom of Saguenay. They had spoken of great quantities of gold and of the people "dressed . . . in cloth like that of white men, and they wore ropes of gold around their necks." [17] Early in September, the explorers reached the home of Donnaconna, the village of Stadacona, situated along the banks of the St. Lawrence River at the site of present-day Quebec City. It was here that Cartier heard local Natives refer to the immediate lands surrounding the river as "Canada." Soon, the French were using the same geographical reference. They gave the bulk of the territory they were exploring on behalf of their sovereign the name La Nouvelle France (New France).

After an emotional reunion with their father, Donnaconna's sons refused to continue upriver with Cartier. Though disappointed, on September 19, the captain headed farther up the river in the pinnance, along with two small longboats. After two more weeks, he reached the Indian village of Hochelaga, situated at the foot of a hill. Cartier named the site Mont Real. One day, a great French city in the New World would stand at the site. From the hilltop, Cartier could see up the St. Lawrence, and he viewed rapids that told him he had not discovered the Northwest Passage. His disappointment was crushing. In addition, the Hochelaga villagers warned the European seamen against continuing farther upriver, where they would come face to face with another group of Native Americans, the dreaded Iroquois, whom the Hochelaga people referred to as "Magua," meaning "eaters of human flesh." With few incentives to do otherwise, Cartier decided to return to France.

The season was already shifting to winter, however, and the French party decided to remain along the river until the spring thaw. The men erected a small fort near the mouth of the St. Charles River, near modern-day Quebec. Later improvements in the military facility included the digging of a surrounding moat and the inclusion of a drawbridge as the only entrance. The fort also sported several of the ships' cannons. That winter,

In September 1535, Jacques Cartier and his party met up with a group of Huron residents of Hochelaga (present-day Montreal), who warned him not to continue up the St. Lawrence for fear of encountering the Iroquois, whom the Hurons referred to as "Magua," or "eaters of human flesh."

Cartier stationed 50 of his men at the fort; the remainder stayed onboard his ships.

The winter proved exceptionally cold, and several of Cartier's men became sick with scurvy, a disease caused by vitamin C deficiency. Eventually, the disease caused such widespread illness and general weakness among the French sailors that only a few were healthy enough for sentry duty. (Only after a local Indian instructed Cartier to treat the disease by having his men drink a tea consisting of boiled evergreen tree leaves did the scurvy come under control.) During those harsh winter months, Cartier and his men heard more stories, this time from Donnaconna himself. The tales were of the wealth of Saguenay, which the chief claimed to have visited. The chief wove elaborate fictions of Saguenay's gold, precious jewels, and abundant spices. "Pointing to the silver chain of Cartier's whistle and the handle of a dagger of copper-gilt dangling at the belt of a sailor, one of the natives made it clear that these metals were to be found in" Saguenay.[18]

Donnaconna's stories worked against him. As the French prepared to leave for home on May 6, 1536, Cartier ordered the chief's capture, along with his two sons and seven other Native Americans. He delivered them to the king of France as both a symbolic present and a guarantee of their cooperation in helping Cartier find Saguenay on his return to the St. Lawrence. None of the 10 captives ever saw their homes in the New World again. Nine of them, including Donnaconna and his sons, died within just a few years in France.

After reaching home by mid-July, Cartier set about preparing for a third trip to the region of the St. Lawrence River. He told Francis I that he would need six ships of 100 tons, plus two smaller vessels: a pair of barques suitable for river sailing. The ships would be stocked with two years of provisions to feed 120 sailors and 150 additional passengers, including "soldiers and mechanics such as carpenters, masons, lime makers, tilemakers, blacksmiths, miners and goldsmiths."[19] He also asked for six priests, three bakers, and two apothecaries, well aware of how much his men had suffered because of a lack of medicinal care.

Again, a French war with the Spanish preoccupied the king, and several years passed before he could focus on future discoveries and potential colonization of the St. Lawrence region and Canada. The search for the Northwest Passage was scrapped, and the new goal was to establish a Canadian colony to provide headquarters and a base for exploration and subjugation of the legendary city of Saguenay. Cartier's plans for his third voyage did not go according to his wishes, however. The king did not consider the old Breton sea captain a suitable governor for a

French colony, so he appointed a friend, a nobleman named Jean-François de la Rocque, sieur de Roberval.

Roberval took so long to organize his colonizing voyage back to North America that Cartier became impatient. He took his portion of the expedition, including five ships, and set sail ahead of Roberval, leaving St.-Malo on May 23, 1541. Roberval's ships did not embark for the Americas for another year. Cartier's third experience in the region of Canada did not go well; it was constantly beset by problems, casualties, and failures. After explaining to Chief Donnaconna's people that their leader had died (Cartier claimed that the others had decided to remain in France), the Breton sea captain pushed up the St. Lawrence River aboard his long-boats and returned to the site of modern-day Montreal. He hired local Native Americans to guide him and his men to legendary Saguenay.

The explorations never reached the fictitious city of wealth. After months of fruitless searching, winter set in and Cartier and his men were forced to experience another grueling and harsh season on the river. During that miserable winter, an Indian attack resulted in the deaths of 35 of Cartier's men. With the arrival of spring, Cartier was ready to leave the region, certain that Saguenay was little more than a gilded myth and that Roberval was not going to join him.

When Cartier reached the mouth of the St. Lawrence, however, he was surprised to discover Roberval's three merchant ships approaching St. John's, Newfoundland. Roberval had 200 colonists, both men and women, onboard, and he was ready to explore. Although Cartier was prepared to continue back to France, Roberval ordered him to remain. Cartier refused, and he soon dispatched his ships, leaving Governor Roberval under cover of darkness. The seasoned seaman returned to France with a cargo of "gold ore" and diamonds his men had uncovered, but it was soon determined that they were neither. The ore was identified as marcasite and the diamonds nothing more than quartz crystals. It would be Cartier's last voyage to the Western Hemisphere. Disappointed, he retired to St.-Malo, where he died in 1557.

Roberval remained in the vicinity of the St. Lawrence River and sought riches of his own. He reached the mouth of the river and established a new fort, where he and his would-be colonists spent a difficult winter: Scurvy and other diseases claimed 50 people, 1 of every 4. Roberval also proved unpopular as a leader, in part because of his harsh rule over his colonists:

> He sat over his people with grimness of judgment. . . . A man named Gailler, one of the malefactors, was detected in theft and promptly hanged. One Jean de Nantes was placed in irons for an infringement of the laws of decency. Women as well as men were sentenced to the whipping post for minor offenses. One member of the party . . . asserts that six men were shot in one day and that the situation became bad enough to win the sympathy of the savages at Stadacona.[20]

By late spring of 1543, Roberval was engaged in a longboat expedition up the St. Lawrence, repeating earlier efforts made by Cartier. He and his people reached the site of modern-day Montreal, but when one of his longboats capsized, resulting in the drowning of all on board, Governor Roberval decided to turn back. He packed up his struggling colony and limped back to France that summer, arriving at St.-Malo in September. With Roberval's return and Cartier's retirement, France's initial efforts at true exploration of Canada, its islands, and the St. Lawrence ended in a whimper, a failure that would not be remedied for two generations. It appeared from their New World efforts that the region offered no immediate riches in gold or diamonds. (In France, anything that appeared genuine but was actually fake became known as "a diamond of Canada.")[21]

The immediate aftermath of these exploratory failures was the effect the French had on the Native Americans in the region. European diseases ran rampant through the Indian villages that Cartier, Roberval, and their followers had visited. As many as 10 epidemics struck various Native American settlements.

Sixty years passed before the French mounted any serious effort to return to the region scouted by Cartier and attempt colonization and settlement again. This new generation of French exploiters came to Canada not in search of gold but to gain riches from a source previously untapped by the Europeans —the fur trade.

The Father of New France

When Francis I dispatched explorers to the New World during the 1530s, he did so with the hope that they would find a route through North America to the fabulous wealth of the Orient or discover gold as the Spanish had in their colonies in Mexico and Central America. Neither hope was realized. What attracted a new generation of French explorers to the region of the St. Lawrence River was a different sort or riches, the wealth represented in the abundance of fur-bearing animals in Canada. Cartier had noted the fur potential in reports of his voyages, but little had been done to tap those resources. Sixteenth-century Englishmen and Frenchmen who sailed to North American waters to engage in the lucrative fishing business sometimes traded New World furs on the side—a second means of making a profit.

Adequate supplies of European-produced fur kept the market saturated. Some American fur, such as beaver, ermine, otter, raccoon, and especially the pelt of the rare black fox, did become highly prized in Europe—one black fox skin sold in London in 1584 for 100 pounds. However, by 1600 the beaver in Europe had nearly been trapped out and were on the verge of extinction. This fact alone led the next generation of French explorers, intent on establishing a significant fur trade with local Native Americans, to return to the St. Lawrence region. In fact, the northern climes of Canada were home to beaver with thicker furs than were common in Europe.

In the late 1500s, French merchants sailed up the St. Lawrence River and began to trade for furs at the Indian trading site at Tadoussac, near where Cartier had wintered, along the terminus of the Saguenay River. The French traded a wide variety of European manufactured goods, including knives, axes, iron kettles, and clothing. One French trader observed how willingly the Indians converted their furs into coveted trade items: "The beaver does everything perfectly well. It makes kettles, hatchets, swords, knives, bread. In short, it

The present-day village of Tadoussac, at the head of the St. Lawrence and Saguenay Rivers and northeast of Quebec City, was France's first trading post in New France, where traders exchanged a wide variety of European manufactured goods, including knives, axes, iron kettles, and clothing for Indian furs.

makes everything."[22] The competition among Indian tribes for French trade goods became so intense that they fought one another for control of the coastal trade. Emerging from this important trade extension of France was a merchant-adventurer named Samuel de Champlain.

Champlain was born along the south coast of Brittany, served in the French army and fought against the Spanish, and was decorated for bravery. In his early years, he sailed to the Caribbean with an uncle and lived in Cuba, Mexico, and Panama for three years. In 1603, by then a world-wise man in his mid-30s, Champlain joined a French effort to establish a trading colony in Canada. The group first scouted the St. Lawrence for a likely location. Champlain relished his arrival in the northlands and was eager to explore them. The region of the St. Lawrence had changed dramatically since the days of Cartier:

> Gone were the tribes which had extended such tempered receptions to the first Frenchmen. Gone was the palisaded city that Cartier had found at Hochelaga. The tall natives who had occupied Mount Royal and its vicinity had been replaced by a few wandering bands of Algonquins. But everywhere [Champlain] heard tales of the great rivers and the gigantic lakes and of the wonder of the country drained by these waters, and he returned to France in the fall more convinced than ever that his lifework was here.[23]

Upon their return to France, they received royal permission to start a colony after recounting their successful mission. The colony's organizer, Pierre de Guast, sieur de Monts, received credit from the French crown for a trading post monopoly for one year and soon gathered a fleet of three ships and 120 men, including Champlain and a pair of clergymen—one Catholic, the other Protestant. Monts sailed as part of a fleet to the north, reached Canada by May 1604, traveled up the St. Lawrence River, and established a trading outpost near Stadacona, the Indian village Cartier had reached, which had since been abandoned by its Native inhabitants. The party called the site "Kebec," from an Algonquian word meaning "where the river narrows."[24] The French economy at home was suffering during these years, but the trading colony prospered from the start. Under the directorship of Monts, the French fur post reaped huge profits from exchange with local Native Americans.

Champlain came to Canada not as a trader but as a soldier and amateur cartographer. He almost immediately began drawing up a detailed map of the coastline of the St. Lawrence River and spent some time searching for a legendary city of gold, Norumbega, which did not exist. Champlain explored the region almost constantly, sometimes looking for a good site for a permanent French settlement, a site with access to the river yet defensible against Indian or even European attack. One of the first sites he selected was situated on the island of St. Croix in St. John's River. Although the location proved defensible, it was not inhabitable because of a lack of freshwater, tillable soil, and adequate stands of timber. At that locale, the French trading colony barely survived its first winter. Snows fell to a depth of four feet, and scurvy killed 35 of the French colonists. The site was abandoned the following spring.

During the next two years, Champlain continued his explorations, trekking up and down the coast of modern-day Maine and Massachusetts looking for a better trading location. During that expedition, in the summer of 1605, Champlain and his men landed along Massachusetts Bay. Fifteen years later, English separatists, popularly known as the Pilgrims, arrived at the same site onboard their famous ship, the *Mayflower*. Near modern-day Boston Harbor, the French met with friendly Indians who were eager to trade with the Europeans. The encounter was fortuitous for Champlain's party because the Natives offered them much-needed food, including small green squashes and pumpkins, which Champlain wrote in his journal made "good salad." [25] A few days later, the Frenchmen encountered another group of Indians who tried to take one of the party's iron kettles. One French sailor was killed in the ensuing skirmish, shot with arrows and stabbed with knives.

The French fired a volley with their guns but did not manage to kill a single Indian. Some of the men wanted to pursue their attackers, but Champlain advised against it, telling them that the Indians could never be caught, "for they ran fast as horses." [26]

By 1607, the same year the English established their first permanent colony at Jamestown, along the Atlantic coast, the French finally settled permanently along the coast of Nova Scotia at a site they called Port Royal. Champlain became extremely excited about the location. The natural harbor, today called the Annapolis Basin, was large enough for more than 1,000 sailing ships.

In the spring of 1607, the fur-trading colony received terrible news from France. The traders and hatters of Paris had petitioned the king to demand that the charter for the trading colony be revoked. These Parisian merchants, who depended on fur from America, swore that they would no longer pay the high prices demanded for New World beaver skins. Their efforts succeeded, and, in August of that year, the colonists of Port Royal and its vicinity, including Champlain, boarded their ships; they reached France by late September.

A RETURN TO THE ST. LAWRENCE

After their return to France, Monts and Champlain met in Paris to discuss the possibility of reestablishing their colony in Canada and, to that end, Monts met with the French monarch, Henry IV. Although the king was sympathetic, he was not prepared to reestablish a monopoly for Monts in the Canadian fur trade. Instead, he offered to renew the French merchant-trader's charter for one more year, but, after that, it would "be a case of every man for himself." [27] With little choice, Monts agreed and soon convinced past investors in the New World trading enterprise to refinance the trading colony. The money raised paid for three small ships, two of which were to sail for the St. Lawrence. Champlain was given command of one of those vessels.

From his first landing in Canada, Champlain had become committed to remaining in North America and playing a significant role in founding a permanent French presence. With his rearrival along the St. Lawrence in 1608, he was about to make his most significant contributions. That June, he met with a tribe along the river, the Montagnais, and gained their permission to establish a colony farther upriver, "near the ruins of the fort occupied by Cartier,"[28] the place called Quebec. When he and his colonists reached the site, where the St. Lawrence narrowed to a width of less than a mile, Champlain instructed his people to set to work. He selected the trees he wanted felled, mostly butternuts, and ordered them sawed into planking for houses. The colonists also dug a root cellar and a common storehouse. Within one month, the site featured "three frame houses, two stories in height and with a three-cornered courtyard in which stood a watchtower."[29] One of the buildings, although built of local materials, featured glazed windows and doors that had been brought over from France. A stout wooden palisade was also constructed around the new buildings to provide security from possible attack; loopholes were included, along with several cannon emplacements. A moat ran along the length of the wooden fence.

With security and defense addressed, Champlain encouraged his people to begin planting crops for food. Everyone planted a garden, including Champlain, who "labored diligently himself with a spade in the space cleared at the west of the fort."[30] Soon, fields of winter wheat, rye, and other Old World crops were planted, ready to be harvested in the spring. The colony struggled through a difficult winter season, however, and many died of scurvy. By April 1609, only 8 of Champlain's 24 settlers were still alive. The colony soon received new colonists, as well as fresh supplies of food, from one of the other French ships sent under Monts' new charter.

As the colony struggled along, Champlain and his colonists became embroiled in an intertribal war that was spreading north and south from the St. Lawrence River. The local Montagnais tribe was allied to upriver Huron Indians, who considered the Iroquois—the Five Nations—enemies. The Iroquois lived to the south, in modern-day New York State. Although wary of getting caught in the middle of these Native American rivalries, Champlain understood that it would be impossible to expand French trade along the St. Lawrence without siding with one Indian group. The French leader had to make a decision. He chose to ally with the Algonquians for two practical reasons: First, he had already established trade relations with the Algonquians, and second, the beaver pelts that the Algonquians brought to Champlain, which they received from their Indian connections far to the north, were thicker than the pelts that the Iroquois brought from farther south.

That summer proved crucial and decisive for Champlain and his colony at Quebec. In June, the French entrepreneur and 12 men, each armed with the crude, short-barreled gun known as an arquebus, set out up the Richelieu River, a tributary of the St. Lawrence, in a small boat. Following the French shallop were "birch-bark canoes in great numbers, all of them filled with the warrior allies of the French, Montagnais, Algonquins, and Hurons," bound for Iroquois country.[31] As the mixed European-Indian war party advanced, Champlain's numbers dwindled. Reaching a great waterfall on the river, the French leader had to send the shallop and several of his men back downriver, keeping only two soldiers to continue the advance. Quarrels among his Indian allies and a growing fear as they pushed farther into Iroquois territory caused several of his Indian allies to abandon him.

Champlain doggedly pushed on. By late July, the party reached the largest freshwater lake Champlain had ever seen,

In the early seventeenth century, French explorer Samuel de Champlain, depicted here in a statue on Nepean Point in Ottawa, Ontario, developed a lucrative trading colony near Stadacona, which his party named "Kebec," an Algonquian word meaning "where the river narrows." Champlain would go on to serve as the unofficial governor of Quebec and would later discover the lake in New York State that bears his name.

which he named after himself. On the evening of June 29, along the lake where a major French garrison, Fort Ticonderoga, would one day stand, Champlain and his men spotted canoes of the Mohawks, one of the Five Nations of the Iroquois. What followed was a strange encounter in the wilderness of North America: "The two parties approached each other openly and a challenge to battle was exchanged in jeering voices across the tranquil water."[32] The Iroquois could not be lured out into the water for a fight, however, choosing instead to go ashore, where they built campfires and began to dance and chant war songs, a scare tactic they kept up throughout the night. Champlain and his allies lashed their canoes together, spending the night in the relative safety of the water.

The next day delivered war to the shores of the remote frontier lake:

> In the morning the three Frenchmen donned their breast-plates, which were so highly polished that they caught the rays of the rising sun and sent fingers of reflected light out across the waters of the lake. Champlain himself donned a casque [helmet] with a white plume as the mark of leadership. The men loaded their carbines and filled the ammunition straps slung across their shoulders. Each of them was equipped as well with sword and dagger. Their fingers were steady and their eyes did not waver as they peered into the depths of the forest where the Iroquois were preparing.[33]

As the Iroquois approached for battle, Champlain soon realized that he was facing as many as 200 warriors, who vastly outnumbered his allies. Leading them were three chiefs carrying stone hatchets. The Frenchmen knew they had an advantage because of their firearms. Native Americans did not yet have access to such weapons, and the arquebuses (matchlock guns) proved vital to the outcome of the day's bloody encounter. As the three chiefs approached, Champlain raised his large-barreled weapon, which was loaded with four bullets, and took aim at the Iroquois chiefs. In a fiery gun blast, a new sight to the Iroquois, Champlain managed to down all three chiefs, killing two instantly. Stunned, confused, and angered, the Iroquois launched a barrage of arrows toward the gathered Hurons. In seconds, one of Champlain's men emerged on the Iroquois flank and fired into a band of warriors, which caused a general panic and retreat. Inspired by the effects of the Frenchmen's gunshots, the Algonquians sprang into action, chasing the fleeing Iroquois with war clubs, hatchets, and scalping knives. They caught several of the enemy, killed them, and managed to capture a dozen warriors. The Iroquois encampment was taken, and the Algonquians seized their enemies' canoes and destroyed them. The battle was over almost as soon as it had begun.

That evening, the Algonquians took one of their captives and tortured him, "tearing out his fingernails, pressing red-hot stones to his writhing limbs, ripping deep strips of flesh from his hide after breaking his bones and exposing the tendons."[34] Champlain wrote how the Algonquians "ordered him to sing [his death song], if he had the heart. He did so, but it was a very sad song to hear."[35] Sickened by the display, Champlain was granted permission to fire a bullet into the suffering warrior.

The quick and decisive victory against the Iroquois brought about by the use of French guns caused the Algonquians to develop a strong alliance with the French, one that would continue for nearly two centuries. Champlain engaged in a second attack against the Iroquois a year later; this attack amounted to little more than a massacre of dozens of Iroquois warriors, with firearms again ruling the day. These encounters may have helped make the Algonquians long-term allies, but they created unsettling memories that the Iroquois would not forget even a century later. For many years, the Iroquois considered the French their mortal enemies, and they harassed French settlements, including the colonial towns of Quebec and Montreal, well into the eighteenth century. Champlain may have won a battle that day, but his deadly work led to a "North American Hundred Years' War." [36]

A STRUGGLING COLONY

During these years, Champlain worked extremely hard to develop Quebec and colonize the St. Lawrence River valley. However, the colony struggled to develop and produce acceptable profits, and in 1611, Champlain made a trip to France to meet with Monts about the colony's slow development. Monts had already invested much of his personal fortune in Canada, though, and his money was nearly depleted. He "transferred to Champlain full power to make such arrangements as he might for the struggling colony and urged him not to desist or lose heart." [37] Champlain set out to find another patron for his New World colony, preferably someone close to the king of France. His efforts took several years of repeated trips between Canada and France.

By 1614, Champlain had found his patron, a nobleman, the Prince de Conde, whose family was one of the most respected in France. The prince agreed to lend the prestige of his name to Champlain's new plans for his St. Lawrence colony; in return he was to receive 1,000 crowns annually. He would not have to immigrate to the New World, but he agreed to send six new families to Quebec each year. Despite several years of colonization on the St. Lawrence, Quebec was home to only a handful of colonists. With this well-known name in hand, Champlain was able to get the merchants doing business in France's most important ports to join in an association with him. The coup of recruiting Conde allowed Champlain to finally return to French Canada and remain there with a renewed confidence in his colony's future.

With Conde's backing, Champlain was able to renew his explorations of the St. Lawrence River valley. He seemed to travel up every river and met with countless villages of Indians. Perhaps his most important exploration took place between 1615 and 1616, when he and a party of Indian guides and friends paddled canoes, "the fleur-de-lis always fluttering at the prow,"[38] up the Ottawa River; portaged to the Mattawa; and finally reached the banks of Lake Nipissing. He continued to Georgian Bay (Champlain was convinced that the bay was one of the "Great Lakes" he had always heard the Natives talk about). Here, he reached a Huron village called Cahiague, "which had two hundred lodges and triple palisades thirty feet high."[39] Champlain's arrival coincided with the Hurons preparing to go to war with the Iroquois. The newly arrived visitors joined in yet another war between Indian tribes, during which Champlain was wounded in the leg by an arrow. The wound, and the fact that Champlain and his men had reached the encampment late that season, forced them to remain at the village through the winter.

Champlain continued to provide solid leadership for Quebec and for French fur-trading efforts along the St. Lawrence. His restructuring of the colony and his deal with Conde soon translated into significant profits, sometimes reaching 40 percent annually. Administering Quebec never became easy for the French colonizer, however. Despite increased profits, investors constantly balked at increased expenses. Some did not appreciate Champlain's leadership and tried to have him removed. In addition, Indian conflicts never came to an end, and the population remained stagnant, with only a small number of new colonists arriving. Even 20 years after Champlain arrived in the region of the St. Lawrence River, the number of colonists in Quebec was still far fewer than 100. By the 1620s, several of Quebec's buildings were beginning to fall into disrepair. In contrast, the English had already established successful colonies with hundreds of inhabitants at Jamestown, Virginia, and in modern-day Massachusetts, with the arrival of the *Mayflower* and the Puritan dissidents.

Champlain remained dedicated to his colony's future, however, and he continued to refuse to "allow his great project to be ruined by the greed of grasping individuals."[40] Despite the slow growth of his colony, he continued to dream of a significant city situated along the banks of the St. Lawrence:

> Champlain's head was filled with plans. He would have a stone citadel on the crest, a series of streets and squares, broad and clean and airy, churches with lofty spires, a hospital. He even dreamed of houses climbing up the steep path, a waterfront of enduring stone; of orderly days and secure nights, and church bells tolling the hours. But he would not live to see the realization of more than a fraction of his fond hopes.[41]

NEW HOPE FOR CHAMPLAIN'S QUEBEC

By the late 1620s, Champlain's Quebec received a new sense of direction and investment. For years, various French monarchs had dabbled with French influence along the St. Lawrence but had never fully committed themselves to the New World venture. In 1627, however, a Catholic bishop, Armand-Jean de Plessis de Richelieu, better known simply as Cardinal Richelieu, became a chief advisor to the young French monarch, Louis XIII. He became convinced that the French colony must be directly administered by the French crown, thus ending years of royal neglect. During the spring of that fateful year, the cardinal created a new trading company for Quebec—the Company of One Hundred Associates. The cardinal's plan was to grant control of North America, including the fur trade, to this new investment group for a term of 15 years. In order to help facilitate trade and encourage profits, all items imported from the St. Lawrence region would have no duties placed on them. In exchange, this new company was to support the immigration of 300 colonists to Canada each year, bringing the total number of French colonists in North America to more than 4,000 within 15 years. If successful, in less than a generation the Company of One Hundred Associates could accomplish a much greater level of growth and development along the St. Lawrence than ever before. (For additional information on this trade group, enter "Company of One Hundred Associates" into any search engine and browse the many sites listed.)

Champlain was ecstatic. Despite the control handed to the One Hundred Associates, he was excited about the formation of a fleet of nearly two dozen ships with hundreds of colonist families onboard—men, women, and children bound for the New World, intent on helping populate Quebec. At last his colony would be justified and recognized as a viable extension of French power. Such development of the colony's resources and potential would, hopefully, counterbalance the increasing presence of the English to the south.

The creation of the One Hundred Associates caused the English to take a more serious look at their French rivals in the north. These rivals of the French had already raided Port Royal as early as 1616. That invasion had been minor, resulting in the capture of about 14 French colonists and the burning of several buildings. The English made an extremely serious strike in the St. Lawrence region in 1628, when three ships under the command of Captain David Kirke reached Quebec. (The ships had been paid for and sent by an English group similar to the French One Hundred—the Company of Merchant Adventurers —which had received word that Richelieu intended to deliver four French warships to the New World.) Kirke arrived off the coast of Newfoundland before the arrival of the French ships and was free to raid at will. Champlain could do little but move the colonists of Quebec into the colony's fort and hope for the

Armand-Jean de Plessis de Richelieu, who is better known simply as Cardinal Richelieu, was instrumental in convincing King Louis XIII that France should focus more on its efforts to develop the trading colony of New France. As a result, Richelieu created the Company of One Hundred Associates, which would enjoy a virtual monopoly on the North America fur trade and a partial monopoly on other trade endeavors in return for transporting at least 4,000 settlers to New France over a 15-year period beginning in 1628.

best. Through the following winter, the colony of Quebec was besieged by Captain Kirke, and many of the men of the colony abandoned the women and children, who were left behind to nearly starve to death. (Only 16 men were left by the spring of 1629.) By August 9, Champlain had no choice but to surrender his colony to the invading English. For the next three years, the English held the settlement of Quebec.

During those years, Champlain lived in Paris, constantly campaigning for the restoration of French influence in Canada. He kept in contact with the directors of the One Hundred, as well as with Richelieu and the French king. Finally, in the spring of 1632, a new treaty formally transferred Canada back to French control. By then, however, the Company of One Hundred Associates was on the verge of bankruptcy. Still, Cardinal Richelieu sent Champlain back to Canada to reestablish a French presence. The old French colonizer made the return voyage to the St. Lawrence River for the last time in the spring of 1633.

The Quebec Champlain returned to was almost unrecognizable:

> The English had burned down the already rickety habitations. The Indians, having been sold alcohol by the English, were indulging in murderous drunken brawls every other night. [But] after the English cleared out, the supply of alcohol was cut off and the Montagnais sobered up; the French forbade selling [alcohol] to the natives under pain of confiscating trading licenses, and the cat o' nine tails.[42]

The local Natives welcomed Champlain and the return of the French. They held a special banquet for him, and an Indian chief gave a speech in which he stated that "when the French were absent the earth was no longer the earth, the river was no longer the river, the sky was no longer the sky."[43] Champlain

(continued on page 56)

THE ROLE OF THE "BLACK ROBES"

From the beginning of his New World colonizing efforts, Samuel de Champlain understood the importance of cultivating positive relations with the Native American population. Their interaction and friendship were crucial to the maintenance of trade between the two cultures. To that end, French colonizers, including Champlain, laid a groundwork of influence on the Native American populations: One focused on diplomacy and trade; the other was about religion.

When the early French trading companies reached the St. Lawrence River region, their traders, buyers, and agents were not especially concerned with the spiritual welfare of the Indians with whom they did business. By the 1620s, however, a significant missionary effort was launched by the Catholic Church and the French crown. Catholic missionaries were sent to the New World by the dozens. Members of various Catholic orders came but most were Jesuits. During the seventeenth century, 115 Jesuits came to French Canada. Among their number were some of the most highly educated young men of Europe. To the Natives with whom they made contact, they became known as the "Black Robes," a reference to the distinctive black garment the Jesuits wore.

These New World ministers did not remain within the French settlements along the St. Lawrence Valley; they scattered across Canada, sometimes pushing into the remote corners of French encroachment. They made connections with many Indian tribes, adapting their gospel message and tactics for their Native American audience. One of their greatest skills was their ability to learn Native languages. Already well-versed in French, as well as Greek and Latin, the Jesuits learned Native dialects to enhance their communication with the Indians. They also used their knowledge of disease to lure converts:

> The Jesuits' most powerful tool was the inability of the Indian shamans to cure the diseases the French brought. Seemingly impervious to chickenpox, mumps, and other illnesses, the Jesuits belittled and insulted the shamans when they tried to cure the sick in traditional fashion. If the Jesuits did not root out the native religion (and indeed,

some were martyred in trying), many natives adopted Catholicism because of the Jesuits' efforts.*

Jesuits lived among the people they wanted to convert and tried to fit into their tribal social structure. They used their knowledge of Indian languages to create stories and analogies to New World Indian life that the Natives would easily understand. At times, they tried to appeal to Native American practices as a means of converting them. The Indian practice of wearing magic charms and amulets was altered by Jesuits who encouraged the Native Americans to wear Christian symbols such as crucifixes.

Sometimes, the Jesuits took advantage of the ignorance and superstition they encountered among the Indians to help convince the Natives that they, as Christian men, had special powers. When a Jesuit father established a mission in a Huron village, he put a clock on display in the newly built chapel. The clock was a mystery to the Natives. They were impressed with the priest's power over the strange ticking device. When the clock struck the eight o'clock hour, the priest, after eight chimes, would shout "Stop!" Such a power did not go unnoticed by the befuddled Hurons. Another Jesuit father, after consulting his almanac, pretended, during an eclipse, to take away the light of the moon. The display frightened his Indian neighbors, giving him great power in their eyes.

The Recollects, the Franciscan "Gray Robes," also came to the New World to preach Christianity to the Indians of French Canada, but their approach did not win them many converts. They did not travel far and establish themselves among Native villages but built schools, hospitals, and churches. They did not adapt their approach to Indian practices and social customs but expected Indians to adapt to European practices and customs, even to the point of abandoning their culture completely. Between 1620 and 1650, the Recollects abandoned their missionary efforts in French Canada, leaving much of the work of Christianizing Indians to the order of religious brothers who were the most successful—the black-robed friars called the Jesuits.

* Hoffer, 320–321.

(continued from page 53)

had returned to the land he had grown to love. He planned punitive raids against the English to the south, the Dutch on Manhattan Island, and the Iroquois, who had remained his bitter enemies. He oversaw the construction of new buildings, including a chapel that he named Notre Dame de la Recouvrance, "Our Lady of Recovery." Champlain was especially excited about the construction of a Jesuit school at Quebec. He continued to deliver letters to Richelieu to ask for more troops to protect Quebec and its residents, and directed the building of a fort at Trois-Rivières, "on a tableland overlooking both the St. Maurice and the St. Lawrence rivers."[44] Although in his mid-60s, Champlain took no rest from the work of rebuilding Quebec. The old colonizer's days ended in October 1635, however, when he suffered a stroke and became paralyzed. He remained restricted to his bed until his death on Christmas Day.

CHAMPLAIN'S LEGACY

The population of Quebec deeply mourned the passing of the colony's founder. Even the Native Americans, those whom Champlain had engaged with in trade for nearly a quarter-century, felt the sorrow of his passing. The following spring, when a group of Huron arrived in the St. Lawrence settlement to trade, they brought along a collection of wampum belts to give to the people of Quebec to "help wipe away their tears."[45] Champlain had been the right man to settle Quebec. From the beginning, he had understood the importance of establishing friendly relations with the Indians, whom the French would rely on for trade. His policies toward the Natives included treating them not only in a friendly manner, but also "respecting their customs and prejudices."[46] Other European colonizers in the Americas, such as the Spanish and Portuguese, became noted for exploiting, enslaving, and destroying Native populations in Central and South America, but Champlain's French colonists developed their colony by living side by side with the Hurons and various Algonquian tribes.

Because Champlain sought mutual benefits for both his people and those who lived on the lands of the St. Lawrence region when the Europeans arrived, the French were able to maintain the development of their colony, including the outpost of Quebec, without destroying the indigenous peoples. In fact, the French and Indians of Canada ultimately intermarried, a development that Champlain once predicted during a diplomatic session with a Montagnais chief: "Our sons shall wed your daughters and henceforth we shall be one people."[47]

Although Champlain gave more than 32 years of his life to the cultivation of French Canada and the settlement of Quebec, he was never honored by the French crown with the appropriate title or official office. He never received the title of governor of New France. His successor, a Maltese knight named Charles de Montmagny, was granted the title even before his arrival in the New World. History would remember Champlain, however, and, in the nineteenth century, bestow on him another, more honorable title, one that addressed the historical contribution of the French leader: father of New France.

5

War along the River

By the year of Samuel de Champlain's death, the French had established themselves firmly in the region of the St. Lawrence River. Their trade relations with the Native Americans were extensive, French fishing ports dotted the Atlantic coastal waters from Labrador to Newfoundland, the Jesuits were ministering to French and Indian alike, and Quebec commanded the heights above the river—the crowning achievement of the long career of the father of New France. Men such as Champlain had spent years exploring the St. Lawrence River, its tributaries, and neighboring bodies of water, and the seventeenth century witnessed even more discoveries by intrepid French adventurers and entrepreneurs.

Even before Champlain's death, a young Frenchman named Étienne Brûlé had blazed new trails across the Canadian landscape. He had arrived in New France with Champlain in 1608 as a teenager who would help establish the frontier settlement of Quebec. Champlain had sent him among the Algonquian peoples to learn their language and serve as an interpreter. Brûlé was a natural wanderer, and during his decades in New France, he traveled far and wide. He explored the Ottawa River, a tributary of the St. Lawrence, and was the first European to reach the Lachine Rapids, as well as Lake Huron, the middle of the five Great Lakes. During the 1620s, Brûlé probably reached Lake Superior, the farthest west of the Great Lakes. He and a companion may have traveled as far as the present-day site of Duluth, Minnesota. Before his explorations were complete, the adventurous Frenchman may have seen all five Great Lakes and was certainly the first European to see Lakes Huron, Ontario, Superior, and Erie.

Despite his travels on behalf of New France, Brûlé turned on his countrymen and helped the English attack the colony of Quebec in 1629, during which Champlain personally surrendered. When the French took back New France three years later, Brûlé left the settlements and returned to live with the Hurons. After a falling out with the Indians, Brûlé was killed, his body was dismembered, and the Hurons ate his remains.

With the reestablishment of New France, the colony experienced new growth and settlement. During the early 1640s, Paul de Chomedey, sieur de Maisonneuve, a nobleman and military veteran, joined an effort to establish a new Jesuit missionary town along the St. Lawrence. Maisonneuve was selected as the party's military leader. The expedition left for the New World on May 9, 1641, and included nearly 40 colonists—among them three women, two priests, and a nurse. A third ship had already left for America. Following the winter of 1641–1642, the French military officer set out in search of a permanent site for the new settlement. Maisonneuve selected a site farther upriver from Quebec, on an island already known as Mont Real. The location was the previous site of Hochelaga, the Huron village Cartier had visited more than a century earlier and that Champlain had found abandoned.

Despite the constant threat of attacks from the Iroquois, the French settlement ultimately succeeded and prospered thanks to the tireless efforts of Maisonneuve, who helped deliver hundreds of new colonists during the colony's first decade. The Iroquois finally signed a treaty of peace with the French at Montreal in 1655. Then, in 1663, the Company of One Hundred Associates was dissolved. Soon, French Canada became a royal colony. King Louis XIV sent French troops to garrison the trade towns and villages, and any further Indian problems (the Iroquois were raiding again by 1663) were dramatically reduced.

COUREURS DU BOIS AND VOYAGEURS

Explorers, settlers, Jesuits, traders, and political officials all made important contributions to the success of New France, but one specialized group was crucial to the future of the French presence in Canada. They were a different breed of

Paul de Chomedey, sieur de Maisonneuve, is depicted here in a statue in downtown Montreal. Chomedey was the founder and served as the first governor of the island of Montreal—an office he held from 1642 until 1663.

French emigrants, those who engaged directly in the fur trade: the *coureurs du bois*, a term that translates as "runners of the woods." These men were the tough, independent-minded agents of trade who traveled deep into Indian country, fanning out in every direction from the St. Lawrence River in search of Indians willing to trade furs for manufactured European goods.

The coureurs du bois shared the New World wilderness of French Canada with a similar group, one whose members were just as hearty and just as determined to tap the fur riches of the North. They were the traders and trappers known as the *voyageurs*, who paddled their canoes into remote areas looking not only for trading partners but also for the furs themselves. One of the most famous of the voyageurs was the legendary French nobleman René-Robert Cavelier, sieur de La Salle, whose river explorations proved that travel by water from the St. Lawrence River to the Gulf of Mexico was possible. Unlike another group of seventeenth-century French immigrants (the farmers, or inhabitants as they were also known), the coureurs du bois and voyageurs were not settlers, nor were they ever settled. They remained out of touch with civilization and village life, moving along river routes for months at a time and returning to settlements such as Quebec, Trois-Rivières, and Tadoussac only when they had trapped or traded enough animal pelts to sell.

By the mid-1660s, the number of French colonists in Canada had reached 3,000. That same decade would witness clashes over the St. Lawrence River valley between its longtime colonizers and the British, who had been busy for nearly half a century colonizing to the south—from colonial New England and New York in the north to the Carolinas in the south. Having largely settled along the Atlantic coast for a couple of generations and having succeeded in seizing colonial outposts held by the Dutch and Swedes in modern-day New York, Pennsylvania, and New Jersey, the British were beginning to eye the teeming fishing villages and developing farming centers, not to mention the always lucrative fur trade of New France, for themselves. To an extent, the developing rivalry between the French and British in North America was part of a greater hostility between the two powers that had been taking place on the European continent for centuries.

The struggle between the French Canadians and the British saw much scattered frontier fighting during the 1680s and 1690s, a conflict the English later referred to as King William's War (1689–1697). The European powers attempted to solicit allies in the various Indian tribes of the region—both concentrating on gaining support from the fierce Iroquois. Ultimately, the Iroquois sided with the British, in part because of memories of the attack against them in 1609 in which Champlain had participated. During the summer of 1689, a large group of Iroquois warriors secretly approached Montreal and attacked the village of Lachine, just a few miles upriver, killing more than 60 people: "With savage brutality they forced helpless women to turn the spit in which their children were roasted to death."[48]

The following spring, Louis de Buade, count of Frontenac, organized more than 1,000 Frenchmen into a series of campaigns, raiding Albany, New York, and Salmon Falls, New Hampshire. British ships followed with retaliation of their own. In March, William Phips, a ship's carpenter born in Maine, convinced the Massachusetts government to support attacks on Canada's Maritime provinces. With 700 men and 14 ships, Phips raided and burned Port Royal and then forced the French residents there to swear an oath of allegiance to Britain. Within two years, Phips was chosen as the colony's first royal governor. Another British colonial move included an attack by a combined force of dozens of New Yorkers and some Iroquois allies on La Prairie on the Richelieu River, across the St. Lawrence from Montreal. Dozens were shot and taken prisoner, and the New Yorkers killed 150 head of French cattle. Before summer's end, Phips laid siege to Quebec and nearly succeeded in causing its fall.

In 1692, the British-allied Iroquois attacked the French village of Verchères, located approximately 20 miles downriver from Montreal, along the St. Lawrence. The siege nearly ended in the collapse of the village, but a 14-year-old girl named Madeleine de Verchères rallied the settlement's inhabitants, oversaw the rationing of food and water, and encouraged her fellow villagers to hold out until French rescuers arrived. For five more years, until France and England signed the Treaty of Ryswick, the raids continued along the St. Lawrence River valley.

King William's War was just one of a series of wars fought between the British and French during the century to follow. Throughout these conflicts, the French understood how important it was to protect the St. Lawrence region in general and the river specifically. War returned to the area in 1702 (the British called the conflict in America Queen Anne's War), and it lasted more than a decade. During this conflict, Massachusetts' militia forces struck at Port Royal in Nova Scotia and captured it in 1710. The result was the passing of French Acadia (present-day Nova Scotia) to British control, "though only nominally, for almost all of its five thousand French and Indian inhabitants refused to take the oath of loyalty to the English Crown."[49]

After the war, in 1713, the French established a new fortress, Louisbourg, on Cape Breton Island, Nova Scotia, to protect the St. Lawrence River (an English fleet had sailed up the river in 1711 to attack Quebec). From this fortified military position, the French could protect against any British fleet entering the St. Lawrence River through the Atlantic Ocean. For the next 30 years, until it was captured by the British in 1745, Louisbourg was the key to protecting New France from further encroachment by sea. The town surrounding the fortress grew quickly,

In 1713, the French established the Fortress of Louisbourg shortly after the end of King William's War. The strategic post was situated on Cape Breton Island, Nova Scotia, to protect the St. Lawrence River from British invasion. The fortress was reconstructed by the Canadian government in the 1960s and has been designated a National Historic Site of Canada.

reaching a population of 700 within two years, and a thriving fishing industry prospered.

By 1745, 4,000 people lived in Louisbourg, and the fortress garrisoned between 1,000 and 1,500 white-uniformed French troops. The French and British were already at war, a conflict known as King George's War (1740–1747), and a British fleet reached the Gulf of St. Lawrence to lay siege to Louisbourg in

NATIVE AMERICAN RESERVES ALONG THE ST. LAWRENCE

During the seventeenth and eighteenth centuries, control of the St. Lawrence River and its surrounding region slipped away from the Native American tribes who had dominated its valley and tributaries for hundreds of years. The French established their control first, then the British government came, only to have the Canadian government become the dominant power in the 1860s. Throughout this process of European rule, the Native Americans—including the Iroquois, Algonquins, Hurons, and others—lost much of their land and a significant portion of their independence along the St. Lawrence.

Native American support of the French placed these Native groups on the wrong side of the British government that came to power in the mid-1700s. The same proved true of Indian tribes in the new United States a generation or two later. Indians were pushed onto U.S. reservations and Canadian reserves, many of which still exist. Many of those reservations and reserves remain today. Several are located along or in proximity to the St. Lawrence; these include the Kahnawake Reserve upriver from Montreal; the Saint Regis Reservation in upstate New York, Quebec, and Ontario; and the Kanesatake Reserve along the Ottawa River, a major tributary of the St. Lawrence. All three provide homes for today's Mohawk Indians.

late spring. After two months, on June 26, the fortress surrendered and the soldiers "marched out carrying their arms and with drums beating and colours flying."[50] Those who surrendered were allowed to emerge from the fort wearing masks so they would not be seen and identified by the locals.

King George's War resulted in other military action along the St. Lawrence River corridor. During the fighting, northern New York and the St. Lawrence River valley "became a no man's land."[51] In 1745, while the French, Hurons, and Abenakis attacked the New York communities of Albany and Saratoga, the British and their Mohawk allies raided up and down the St. Lawrence. Even after the official end of the

Most unique among these reservation lands is the Saint Regis Reservation. The 22 square miles of Indian-owned land stretches across the St. Lawrence River in both New York State and Quebec and Ontario. The Mohawks at Saint Regis select their own tribal councils on both sides of the river. The reserve is home to approximately 13,000 Mohawk people. With the reserve split between two countries, the residents' lives are sometimes different. During the Vietnam War, Mohawk men living on the U.S. side were called into military duty, whereas their relatives on the north side of the St. Lawrence were exempt from duty. Some Canadian Mohawks, however, chose to join the tribal council on the American side and then enlisted in the U.S. military service.

The Kahnawake Reserve sits along the south bank of the St. Lawrence River, on a site once occupied by Fort St. Louis. Many of the Akwesasne Mohawks (Akwesasne means "land where the partridge drums") are the ancestors of Native Americans who converted to Roman Catholicism. Today, Catholic services are performed on the reserve, where "Roman Catholic priests have sung the church liturgy in the Mohawk language for several centuries."* Although today the mass is performed in English, some of the prayers are still spoken in Mohawk.

* Hanmer, 27.

conflict in 1747, Indians allied to the French brought captives to Montreal to be ransomed.

These early conflicts between the British and French—King William's, Queen Anne's, and King George's Wars—were always limited conflicts with limited results. Nothing ever seemed permanent after these military campaigns, which first might witness British victories and gains, only to be followed by French successes. This seesaw series of wars changed little in the region of the St. Lawrence. The wars proved inconsequential overall, with little territory exchanged. In the 1750s, however, a war of great consequence ripped through the Americas, including the St. Lawrence River region.

THE FRENCH AND INDIAN WAR

Unlike the three previous intercolonial international conflicts, the war of the 1750s was destined to be different. The war was not just an extension of a conflict that began on the European continent. Second, the Iroquois had willingly fought alongside the British in early conflicts, but they had grown to mistrust their English allies, leading many tribes to support the French. The British had repeatedly established new towns and cities rather than trading posts, and had created farms, raising long fencerows that removed lands from Indian use. The French had always remained tied to the fur trade—an economic endeavor in which Native Americans had always participated.

The French and Indian War lasted from 1754 to 1763. The conflict raged across the eastern portion of the North American continent from the St. Lawrence to Florida. It was ostensibly a war over which European power would control the vast regional riches of the Ohio Valley, south of the Great Lakes. The French delivered 19 ships and 6 regiments of regular troops to Canada in 1755, and the British sent 2 regiments to Virginia that same year. During the war, much of the lakes region south of the St. Lawrence saw significant fighting as the British and French fought over control of one another's scattering of forts, including the French-built Fort St. Frederic, which was armed with 40 cannons; Fort Carillon on the northern end of Lake George; and the British outposts at Fort William Henry and Fort Edward. (For additional information on this British fort, enter "Fort William Henry" into any search engine and browse the many sites listed.)

During the early years of the war, the French military performed well and succeeded in taking several British forts, including Fort William Henry. French commander General Marquis Louis de Montcalm, "a career officer and a slight, short figure of poise, grace, gentility, and quick wit,"[52] proved a formidable leader: During the Fort William Henry siege in 1757, Montcalm assembled 1,000 Indian allies; more than 3,000 French infantry troops, including 600 troupes de la marine; and an additional 2,600 Canadian militiamen.

Despite such French victories, by 1758–1759, the British began to gain the upper hand. A new British prime minister, William Pitt, altered the crown's commitment to the war and delivered thousands of fresh troops to the front. Soon, the British were directing their war effort along the St. Lawrence. Louisbourg was targeted immediately:

> The door was the Saint Lawrence River, and its hinge was the French fortress of Louisbourg. The colonists had taken it once, but it had been returned to the French in the Peace of 1748. The British assembled a fleet of thirty-eight warships, including twenty ships of the line, the biggest in the British navy, and one hundred transports carrying twelve thousand soldiers to join forces with a smaller fleet at Halifax, Nova Scotia. The French [at Louisbourg] surrendered on July 17, after a month of bombardment.[53]

The fall of Louisbourg was orchestrated by Brigadier General James Wolfe, an "awkward, ungainly man and . . . a hypochondriac"[54] in his late 30s. Wolfe was a capable military commander, and he was soon tapped to carry out a task almost considered impossible: to bring about the fall of Quebec.

As a military target, Quebec would prove difficult to take. Its location on high bluffs above the north banks of the St. Lawrence gave it a commanding view and control of the river. Any army approaching the French town from the St. Lawrence could be spotted easily. The river's bluffs were considered insurmountable, towering 1,800 feet high. In addition, the city hosted a garrison of troops that out-numbered General Wolfe's men 15,000 to 12,000. These advantages, however, would not deter a general as dedicated and professional as Wolfe.

Wolfe's command included some of Britain's best fighting units. (Many serving under the French commander, General Montcalm, were no more than local French-Canadian conscripts.) As he prepared to launch his campaign against Quebec, Wolfe first placed artillery batteries on the river opposite the Quebec cliffs. He then dispatched nearly a dozen ships past the French guns guarding Quebec. With troops and ships strategically placed both upriver and downriver from the French fortress, Wolfe gained control of the St. Lawrence by June 1759. However, he still needed to approach Quebec by way of the cliffs along the St. Lawrence. For days, he studied the cliffs "dressed as a common soldier examining every foot of the steep cliffs opposite his encampment,"[55] while 3,000 French troops patrolled the high ground above the river. From his vantage point, the British general observed a narrow, winding road that scaled the cliff near a small bay known as the Foulon. By day, local washerwomen used the path to bring their laundry from the heights to the river's edge. Perhaps the path could be scaled by his men, resulting in a blow where the French might least expect it:

> Wolfe's plan was to lead an advance force silently for the three or four miles from the ships at Cap Rouge to The Foulon, to halt there and wait while a few men scaled the heights in the darkness. If they reached the top, they could probably hold it while the others climbed up to join them. The few [French guard] tents observed from the other side of the river made Wolfe believe that the guard at the top was weak. It was indeed.[56]

The date for the assault up the cliffs along the St. Lawrence was set for September 13. That morning, Wolfe ordered

24 volunteers up the cliff path to subdue the French guards on the heights:

> If they succeeded, the road up the cliff a few hundred feet to the west, could be quickly cleared and men and artillery brought up . . . The complex effort was worked out with masterly precision; and by eight o'clock about four thousand five hundred British soldiers were taking up their chosen positions on the Plains of Abraham . . . The surprise was complete.[57]

By six o'clock that morning, the British army under Wolfe's command reached the heights known as the Plains of Abraham, just a mile or so from Quebec. To avoid a siege, an astonished Montcalm met Wolfe's forces on the plains. The two European armies—the British in the red uniforms and the French in their stark white—stood opposite one another. Wolfe's men were ordered to charge, and the French troops soon unleashed a musket volley that tore through the English line. Doggedly and patiently, the British held their fire until they were only 20 yards from the French and then opened their own volley, causing the French to run from the battlefield. In the short yet decisive battle, Montcalm was immediately killed and Wolfe took two wounds, the second fatal. The battle was over nearly before it began. Within four days, the French surrendered the jewel of the St. Lawrence—Quebec.

The British advance along the Canadian river continued through the following year, and Montreal fell on September 7, 1760, just one week shy of the anniversary of Quebec's fall. The war dragged on for another three years. The French signed a peace treaty in Paris in 1763, resulting in the transfer of Canada to the British. After 150 years of exploration, exploitation, settlement, and Christianizing, the great French colonizing experiment in the northlands of Canada came to an end. French forts were transferred to British control. Many former French subjects were allowed to remain, however, and the region of the St. Lawrence, including the vast modern-day province of Quebec, remained extensively influenced by French culture and language.

THE AMERICAN REVOLUTION

With the transfer of Canada into British hands, French influence on North America in general and the St. Lawrence River specifically changed forever. Gone were the days of official French dominance and trade throughout the region, although some French trappers and traders continued their work under contract to British agents. Power struggles between the French and British had dominated the region for a century prior to the French and Indian War, but the politics of the region soon shifted and new conflicts emerged. To the south, the British in the 13 colonies along the Atlantic coast soon turned against their mother country and engaged in a rebellion that centered on taxation and arbitrary control exerted by the British crown. By April 1775, American patriots were at war with the British. Although British-controlled Canada had no direct role in the struggle that came to be known as the American Revolution, the region of the St. Lawrence saw a renewal of warfare as the Americans launched a campaign to wrest Canada from British dominance.

The war between the American colonials and the British was barely two months old when the Second Continental Congress authorized a military campaign to the north against the British presence in Canada, "if . . . it will not be disagreeable to the Canadians."[58] Some Americans believed that the St. Lawrence River region could become a fourteenth colony of America. Although thousands of British troops had been stationed in the American colonies throughout the late 1760s and early 1770s, the British had garrisoned perhaps as few as 700 redcoats in

Canada under the command of General Guy Carleton. American military leaders organized a two-pronged attack aimed at capturing both Montreal and Quebec, the same towns the British had targeted during the French and Indian War.

The American commanders appointed to lead the main column of American troops north were General Philip Schuyler and his second in command, Irish-born General Richard Montgomery, a former British officer who had fought in the St. Lawrence region during the French and Indian War. They were to move north along the Champlain Valley, seize the British garrison of St. John's and Fort Chambly along the way, and then advance on Montreal. After capturing the town, they were to move downriver to Quebec. As part of a diversionary tactic, another American unit, under the command of Benedict Arnold, who would later gain infamy as a turncoat, was to march through the northern backcountry of Maine and land downriver from Quebec. The plan was bold, and its success hinged on both armies reaching their goals before the onset of winter.

Unfortunately, Schuyler proved slow in setting out on his leg of the mission. He dallied through much of the summer of 1775, adding new recruits to his army, collecting supplies, building transport boats, and negotiating with the Iroquois for peaceful passage across their lands. When Schuyler became ill, Montgomery took command of his forces and, urged by General George Washington, set out on August 28, 1775, bound for Montreal. The campaign set out on water as a

> strange flotilla, cobbled together out of almost no proper materials, but with a great deal of energy and hope, pushing north down [Lake] Champlain from the shaky American base at Ticonderoga . . . shoving off toward the mysterious immensity of Canada, with the Green Mountains dusk-cloaked on their right and the Adirondacks catching the last flecks of sunset gold on their left.[59]

His army made rapid progress across northern New York, but when Montgomery and his men reached St. John's, the resulting siege against the 500 British troops inside the garrison took eight weeks. By the time the garrison surrendered on November 3, cold temperatures were already beginning to plague Montgomery's army. Despite the arrival of winter, however, the Americans moved on, and within 10 days of the fall of St. John's, Montreal also fell, surrendering without a fight. Unfortunately for the Americans, General Carleton escaped from Montreal and set out downriver to Quebec to help organize its defense.

Montgomery delayed his advance by two weeks, allowing his men to rest and recover from the difficult march into Canada. In the meantime, General Arnold reached the outskirts of Quebec on November 8, but his army was in poor condition. The march through the thick wooded regions of Maine had nearly defeated his men. The advance had been forced to pass repeatedly through frigid swamp water and engage in exhausting portages around several rivers. Food became so scarce during the winter that Arnold's men nearly starved and "at one point [had] been reduced to living on boiled candles and roasted moccasins."[60] In fact, "Captain Dearborn's huge black dog disappeared into a cook-pot."[61] By the time Arnold's forces reached the St. Lawrence, his men were weary, hungry, sick, and nearly unfit for battle. When Montgomery and Arnold reconnoitered in December, only about 1,000 men in the two armies were ready for duty. Nevertheless, the commanders decided to launch a night attack against Quebec and its defenders on December 30.

The British forces in the town were ready and prepared for the attack. The streets were thick with snowdrifts as the Americans advanced. Arnold, personally commanding no more than 650 men, slipped past the Quebec gates and into town, where he and his forces came under immediate fire. Americans

American General Richard Montgomery, a former British officer who served in the French and Indian War, joined Benedict Arnold in leading American troops in the unsuccessful Quebec campaign, which was designed to protect the northern frontier from the British. Montgomery captured Montreal in November 1775, but by December, Continental troops had been decimated by illness, lack of supplies, and desertion, and were unable to capture Quebec City. This painting, titled *The Death of General Montgomery*, depicts Montgomery's demise.

began to fall, and Arnold took a serious bullet wound to the leg. Heavy street fighting ensued, and Montgomery was killed. Although the Americans were able to capture and occupy several houses in the town, the British launched a counter-attack, driving their opponents out during house-to-house engagements. Perhaps as many as 400 Americans were killed or wounded during the night skirmish and another 400 taken prisoner. The Continentals who escaped from Quebec fled into the face of an advancing snowstorm. The British did not even pursue them.

The American campaign into the St. Lawrence Valley was a miserable failure. Montgomery was dead, and Arnold's leg was shattered, resulting in a lifelong limp. The few hundred men who survived the assault sat out the winter in Canada (the British did not bother to drive them back to their colonies until spring). Arnold's men experienced an excruciating winter, fighting both the cold and an outbreak of smallpox "ten times more terrible than Britons, Canadians, and Indians together."[62]

The following spring, the Second Continental Congress dispatched another army, under the command of General John Thomas, north. Soon after his arrival near Quebec, British ships arrived with reinforcements. Thomas retreated to Montreal, but a new outbreak of smallpox killed many Americans, including Thomas. With Thomas' failure and Arnold's ragtag army driven south by a British force under the command of General "Gentleman" John Burgoyne, the American campaign to take control of Canada appeared impossible. Before the end of spring 1776, General Washington finally informed the Congress that the campaign was "almost over."[63]

The campaign to take control of Canada from the British was not the last time the United States attempted to seize the region of the St. Lawrence. During the War of 1812, which brought the new United States government and the British into yet another New World conflict, a group of young American congressmen called the "War Hawks" spoke in support of another punitive campaign into Canadian soil. However, fighting never took place in Canada; the war ended with the Treaty of Ghent in 1815 and no land was exchanged. From that date on, the governments of British Canada and the United States recognized that "the wealth of the St. Lawrence River could be tapped by both countries peacefully."[64] However, another generation would pass before a joint British-American agreement clearly established the true border between the two countries. In 1842, the Webster-Ashburton Treaty set the St. Lawrence River as a part of the border between the two nations. Over the years that followed, the Americans and Canadians (Canada gained its independence from Great Britain in 1867) established friendly relations and cooperated extraordinarily over the two nations' use of the St. Lawrence River.

6

Recreating the River

After the American Revolution, the St. Lawrence River region experienced a new period of growth, development, and change. Significant numbers of people immigrated to the St. Lawrence Valley. Between 1780 and 1800, 500,000 new residents reached the river region. Many came from the new United States as Loyalists who had not supported the patriot cause during the Revolution and settled in modern-day Ontario. Even today, some Canadians who are descended from these Loyalists use the initials U.E. following their surnames; the letters stand for "Unity of the Empire."

The British government of Canada created new provincial divisions as the eighteenth century drew to a close. British Canada was divided into Upper Canada (modern-day Ontario) and Lower Canada (modern-day Quebec) in 1791. Despite the official presence of the British in formerly French Canada, French influences did not die out. Instead, two regions developed. Ontario was most affected by British laws, customs, traditions, and the English language, and Quebec remained predominantly French. The official language of Quebec today is French, and three out of every four people living in Montreal speak the language.

Despite the permanent presence of French influences along the St. Lawrence, a new, British-influenced nation—the Confederation of the Dominion of Canada—was created in 1867. It was formed when the provinces of Nova Scotia, New Brunswick, Quebec, and Ontario agreed to unite. In the early days of the Dominion, the St. Lawrence River continued to determine even the politics of the young Canadian government. No permanent capital was selected immediately; it moved back and forth between Montreal and Toronto. This arrangement was unmanageable, and the Canadians eventually allowed Queen Victoria to select a permanent site for their national capital. She avoided choosing either city and instead selected a small community on the Ottawa River, a major tributary of the St. Lawrence. Today, the city of Ottawa remains the capital of Canada.

The St. Lawrence River had been important during nearly two centuries of influence exerted by the colonists of New France, and it continued as an even greater highway of commerce during the late eighteenth and early nineteenth centuries. By 1830, immigrants were arriving in British Canada, passing through Quebec at the rate of 30,000 annually. With the development of more extensive usage of the river, the nineteenth century brought many changes in the course and nature of the river itself. Much of the St. Lawrence was a gently flowing, smooth river; its course included challenging rapids that made trade and passage on the river, especially upriver between Montreal and Lake Ontario, where there were 200 miles of rapids, difficult—if not dangerous. Even before the nineteenth century, European residents of the St. Lawrence Valley sought ways to bypass these rapids through the construction of man-made waterways such as canals.

THE LACHINE CANAL

As early as 1670, Father François de Salignac of Montreal proposed the excavation of a canal between Montreal and Lachine. His dream of a canal never became reality, but upon his death, his successor, a young French Jesuit priest named François Dollier de Casson, laid out plans for the construction of a mile-long canal that would allow small boats to bypass the Lachine Rapids, upriver from Montreal. Father de Casson spent several years planning his canal project and work began in the late 1680s.

Progress was slow and ultimately hampered by local Iroquois Indians, who considered the man-made alteration of the St. Lawrence an affront to the river. In 1689, Iroquois warriors attacked the settlement of Father de Casson, killing 200 residents. Work on the canal continued for more than a decade, but the canal was only excavated to a length of 2,000 yards, much of it out of solid rock. By 1701, the year of de Casson's death, interest in the canal had waned and available funds had been exhausted. The unfinished canal was abandoned, and the St. Lawrence's Lachine Rapids continued to represent a hazard to human traffic on the river.

Seventy-five years passed before the British began to seriously consider building a canal again. The American Revolution provided incentive for the construction of a canal, because British officials understood the difficulties their military forces faced in moving along the St. Lawrence; particularly around the Lachine Rapids, where troop movements would slow considerably. Soon, a series of small canals was under construction to help bypass not only the rapids of Lachine but additional rapids and cataracts on the river. These canals were extremely narrow, accommodating only small rivercraft. Larger boats, such as barges and later paddle wheelers, could not use the limited canalways and were forced to "shoot the rapids," a harrowing experience "giving their passengers a memory for life." [65] One such passenger wrote of a trip he took through the Lachine Rapids:

> Everybody crowds toward the bows, to watch the big ship lunge down the boiling flood. We can see the great breakers heaving and tossing . . . and in one moment more we are on the Rapids. What shall I say of the sensation? My wife, who is a venturesome body, was disappointed. She wanted a bigger fall, a more sensational leap, and a greater chance of getting her neck broken. But . . . I found the waves quite big enough and fierce enough to make my heart jump a little against my watch-pocket, and my breath catch again in my throat at each respiration. [66]

With the approach of the nineteenth century, the new drive for canal construction focused on the expansion of cargo trade on the river. Canadian goods bound for foreign ports needed a water route to the Atlantic. By 1817, the Americans were busy building the Erie Canal, which ran west to east, across central New York State. The canal was intended to connect Buffalo, New York, on Lake Erie, with the Mohawk River and Albany on the Hudson River, a south-flowing river that reaches New York City. If the Americans constructed a canal, Canadian water trade would be siphoned from the Great Lakes region to the Erie Canal, causing the St. Lawrence to support less trade. Panicky Montreal merchants supported the construction of a Canadian canal to help ensure that their city would became one of the important centers of North American trade.

Construction began on a new Lachine Canal in 1821 and was finished four years later, at the same time the Erie Canal was completed and opened for business. The first completed canal allowed the passage of small, flat-bottomed sailboats. As boat sizes increased and the amount of shipping tonnage rose, however, the Lachine Canal had to be enlarged; the projects taking place between 1843 and 1848 and then from 1873 to 1884. By the mid-nineteenth century, the Lachine Canal was a link in a chain of canals built to develop and encourage shipping trade between Montreal and the Great Lakes. The system was used extensively throughout the late nineteenth century, and by 1929, nearly 15,000 ships were passing through the Lachine's locks annually. Thirty years later, the Lachine was replaced by the St. Lawrence Seaway.

THE WELLAND CANAL

The Lachine Canal helped eliminate the challenge to navigation presented by the Lachine Rapids, but there were other natural obstacles connected to trade and shipping on the St. Lawrence. The most daunting obstacle to trade between the St. Lawrence and the Great Lakes was Niagara Falls. Today the most famous waterfalls in North America, the Niagara system is much more

Though smaller canals were built in the area of the Lachine Rapids, between the Island of Montreal and the south shore of the St. Lawrence River, construction on the Lachine Canal didn't begin until 1821. The canal, shown here in an 1859 photograph, was built in response to the Erie Canal and was used until 1959, when South Shore Canal replaced it.

than rapids: It is a 167-foot drop in elevation between Lakes Ontario and Erie. Overall, the difference in lake levels between Ontario and Erie is more than 300 feet, running along a geologic shelf known as the Niagara Escarpment. Seventeenth- and eighteenth-century French fur trappers and traders, as well as Indians long before them, had been forced to portage their canoes around the falls as they paddled from one lake to the other.

Just four years after the opening of the Lachine Canal, another canal system was completed; it allowed inland ships to circumvent the treacherous, previously impassable Niagara Falls. The man who first dreamed of the project was a Canadian merchant, politician, and developer named William Hamilton Merritt. Born in 1793 in New York State, Merritt was the son of a U.E. Loyalist who had fought for the British during the American Revolution. The revolution had driven the Merritt family from New York into Upper Canada, where they settled in the Niagara district. William Merritt grew up Canadian and proved an intelligent, resourceful youth, forming a partnership in a general store at age 17. He served under British command during the War of 1812, participated in the capture of Detroit, and was taken prisoner after the battle of Lundy's Lane.

After the war, he formed another merchant partnership in the rapidly developing settlement area of St. Catharines, where he speculated in land and developed a local salt spring. As a young man in his early 20s, he began to develop a plan for building a canal that would connect Lakes Ontario and Erie. In 1818, he made a survey of the route for a canal, which he proposed to the Upper Canada legislature the following year. The proposal was a petition signed by several prominent citizens of St. Catharines. The legislators appropriated 2,000 pounds for another survey (Merritt was only an amateur surveyor), while Merritt began raising other monies for the project. Despite his family's Loyalist connections, the entrepreneurial Canadian even traveled to New York City to recruit American investors. He formed a development firm called the Welland Canal Company, named after the Welland River, which ran parallel to a portion of Merritt's proposed canal route. By 1824, the money had been raised and construction on the Welland project began on November 24. Five years later to the month, the canal was complete. (For additional information on the father of the Welland Canal, enter "William Hamilton Merritt" into any search engine and browse the many sites listed.)

The building of the Welland Canal was a difficult and labor-intensive project. Merritt had envisioned his water staircase as a system of 40 locks. The canal ran from Port Dalhousie to Twelve Mile Creek to Port Robinson, where it connected with the Welland River. (The Welland flows as a tributary of the Niagara River, exiting to Lake Erie.) Most of the canal's construction was done by low-paid immigrant workers using little more than picks and shovels. These men were paid about 50 cents a day for their work, which included not only the excavation of a 7-foot-deep and 20-foot-wide canal but also required extensive tree and rock removal. The initial canal was completed in 1829, and the man-made system was augmented between that year and 1833, when five additional locks were built, a water feeder canal was added, and a more direct route from Port Robinson to Port Colborne was constructed. The total cost of this important nineteenth-century canal project was $8 million. When the canal came online, trade and passenger schooners could pass through the system, extending the economic reach of the St. Lawrence River farther across the Great Lakes.

Welland's dream soon became a financial and commercial success. The Canadian developer did not rest on his canal's success, however. Over the next 20 years, Merritt raised monies for the construction of the Niagara Suspension Bridge across the Niagara Gorge (completed in 1845) and helped develop the Welland Railway Company, which ran along his canal and provided freight and passenger delivery through the winter months, when the weather closed the canal. He became involved in Canadian politics, serving in the United Canada legislature from 1841 to 1860. He died in 1862 onboard a ship in the St. Lawrence Canal, a fitting end to a person who helped develop canal trade throughout the river's region. At his death, he was remembered as the father of the Welland Canal.

Over the century that followed, the Welland Canal underwent several key changes and improvements. Its second expansion began in 1842 and was completed in 1845; during these expansions, the Welland's locks were enlarged to a width of 25 feet and received an additional foot of depth to accommodate larger ships. The redesigned canal also reduced the number of locks from 40 to 27. By the completion of this second Welland Canal, direction and control of the system had passed from the Welland Canal Company to the Canadian government.

The Welland Canal was augmented again in 1887 to take a more direct course from Port Dalhousie to Allanburg, abandoning the Twelve Mile Creek leg of the former canal. This new canal system no longer needed its feeder canal as a water source; instead, water was supplied directly from Lake Erie. The revamped canal abandoned 1 of its 27 locks, and the remaining locks were enlarged to a width of nearly 45 feet. The length of the locks was augmented to more than 240 feet. The last significant changes to the Welland Canal took place between 1913 and 1932. Through several stages of change, the canal reached its maximum depth of nearly 30 feet. As the length of the locks increased (today, the Welland locks are nearly 900 feet in length), the number was reduced from 26 to 8, with an average lift of 46 feet. These locks allowed ships 80 feet wide, more than 800 feet in length, and with a draft of 30 feet to bypass Niagara Falls. This increase in lock size would allow the passage of most of the world's ocean freighters. Today, an average passage through the Welland Canal takes 11 hours.

The significance of the Welland Canal in its many forms was and continues to be the expansion of shipping along the water corridor between the St. Lawrence River and the Great Lakes. Today, the canal allows for the transportation of ships carrying massive quantities of a variety of goods, including vast amounts

The Welland Canal, which connects Lake Erie with Lake Ontario, was built to help ships bypass Niagara Falls. Completed in 1829, the canal was the idea of William Hamilton Merritt, who would go on to serve in Canada's legislative assembly and was the country's commissioner of public works from 1850 to 1851. Shown here is a grain boat passing under a railway lift bridge on the canal.

THE MOHAWK: MEN OF STEEL

Today, tens of thousands of the descendants of Native American tribal groups live in the region of the St. Lawrence River. Indian reservations, such as the Saint Regis Reservation in upstate New York and the Kahnawake (Caughnawaga) Reserve near Montreal, even border the banks of the river. As some modern-day Native Americans in the region of the St. Lawrence have struggled to find their place in a world dominated by non-Indians, one group of Indian laborers has served in a unique and dangerous profession—as high-elevation construction workers.

Throughout the early twentieth century, Indian steelworkers proved extremely adept and skillful working on skyscrapers. According to many, they enjoyed the freedom of working up high, with no walls or restrictions. As cityscapes such as New York added to their skylines prior to World War II, many Native Americans, especially Mohawk Indians, worked on such important symbols of New York as the RCA Building, Rockefeller Center, and the Empire State Building, which rose a quarter-mile up from 34th Street in midtown Manhattan.

Before the steel industry lured Indian workers, however, there was the lure of iron. Beginning in the late nineteenth century, Native American men often went into the ironworks profession. In 1886, Mohawk ironworkers were employed by the Canadian Pacific Railroad to build a bridge across the St. Lawrence River near Montreal. The Dominion Bridge Company was required to hire Native American workers because the south end of the bridge reached the Kahnawake Indian Reserve. The Mohawk workmen performed so well that word quickly spread through the industry. As one Dominion official summed it up, "Putting riveting tools in the Mohawk's hands was like putting ham with eggs. They were natural-born bridgemen."*

of grain, iron ore, and coal. In an average year, 1,000 ocean-going ships and 2,500 lake vessels pass through the canal. The total cargo tonnage transported through the Welland Canal usually tops 65,000,000 metric tons annually. In addition to serving as a link in trade from river to lakes, the Welland provides water for industrial production in the greater Niagara

Soon Mohawk workers were employed on construction of the Sault Sainte Marie Bridge in northern Michigan. On that building site, one Mohawk fell to his death. Others died similarly during the decades to follow. In 1890, ironworking was known as the construction industry with the highest mortality rate.

The greatest high-elevation tragedy that involved Native American iron-workers took place in 1907, when the Quebec Bridge collapsed while under construction. The bridge was being built over the St. Lawrence River, nine miles upriver from Quebec City. The planned bridge was to be 1,800 feet in length—then the longest cantilever bridge in the world. Early on the morning of August 29, 1907, men working on the bridge "heard rivets start to pop and felt enormous steel girders twist beneath them."[**] As the mass of steel gave way, nearly 100 workers fell to their deaths. One-third of them, 33 in all, were Mohawks from the Kahnawake Reserve. That loss of life was so sudden and tragic that the Mohawk people still refer to the Quebec Bridge collapse as "the disaster."[***]

Despite the loss of life, the disaster did not deter other Native American men from becoming high-elevation iron and steelworkers. As one Mohawk iron man said, "Instead, it made high steel much more interesting to them. It made them take pride in themselves that they could do such dangerous work."[†] To honor their dead, Mohawk peoples erected a giant iron cross at the Kahnawake Reserve—fashioned from iron girders similar to those used to construct the Quebec Bridge.

[*] *Realm of the Iroquois* (Alexandria, Va.: Time-Life Books, 1993), 163.
[**] Ibid., 164.
[***] Ibid.
[†] Ibid.

region, including filling the needs of steel mills, shipyards, paper mills, and automobile parts production plants. William Merritt himself intended the Welland to provide a consistent source of water for local mills in the early nineteenth century. Today, the canal generates electricity at a small power plant, and it provides recreation for thousands of tourists and boaters in the lakes region. The modern-day legacy of the St. Lawrence River as a major North American trade corridor is partly due to the existence of the Welland Canal.

CONSTANT CHANGE ALONG THE RIVER

Throughout the nineteenth century, improvements and changes in inland shipping lanes and access routes altered the nature of commercial trade along the St. Lawrence: Ships that reached the Gulf of St. Lawrence were increasingly able to access each of the five Great Lakes. Oceangoing sailing ships could travel as far inland as Lakes Huron and Michigan before the mid-1800s. By the 1850s, relations between the United States and Canada were changing the future of the St. Lawrence River and the Great Lakes:

> By the middle of the nineteenth century, the friendship between the United States and Canada meant that the St. Lawrence River had lost its military significance. At the same time, the economic importance of the river was growing dramatically. Lumber had replaced fur as the leading product of the Canadian north woods, and a way was sought to ship lumber products and other raw materials from Canada directly to Europe and the growing midwestern cities of the United States. If this could be accomplished, inland ports like Montreal, Quebec City, Buffalo, and Cleveland could become centers of international trade.[67]

The further internationalization of St. Lawrence River trade would reach new heights over the coming years. Once a series of dangerous rapids at Sault Ste. Marie were bypassed after the building of the Soo Canal in 1856, ocean vessels could finally pass from Lake Michigan to the westernmost lake, Superior. Much of the 1850s canal system from the St. Lawrence to the Great Lakes could accommodate boats and ships with a

9-foot draft, but the Soo Canal was no sooner finished than the need to transit even larger ships, those with a draft of 14 feet, was required. Before 1870, all the canals in the chain of man-made waterways had been altered to such a depth—but even larger ships loomed in the St. Lawrence River's future.

Extensive improvements on the various canals served by the St. Lawrence River in the east and the Great Lakes in the west did not take place overnight. Even as late as 1908, ships that drew more than 14 feet of water were unable to pass from Montreal into the Great Lakes system. Passage along the canal system was long, tedious, and slow and included many lock transfers. The cargoes onboard oceangoing ships too large to navigate farther inland than Montreal had to be offloaded there and reloaded onto smaller river and lake freighters. With the United States and Canada both intent on continuing to encourage further expansion of cargo trade between the Atlantic Ocean and the Great Lakes, a plan of singular scope began to take form. The river could accommodate large ships from the Gulf of St. Lawrence to Montreal, as could the Welland Canal. It was the middle leg, the part of the St. Lawrence from Montreal to the Welland that was inadequate for large ship traffic. A massive waterway construction project, beginning in the mid-1950s, would eliminate this final impediment to the ever-expanding commercial traffic along the modern St. Lawrence River.

7

The St. Lawrence Seaway

The twentieth century would witness one of the greatest waterway construction projects in North America. Although construction on the man-made waterway that would one day be known as the St. Lawrence Seaway did not begin until the mid-1950s, discussion between the United States and Canada concerning a joint, international venture to deepen the existing canals, as well as the St. Lawrence River itself, first took place officially in 1895.

The idea of a "seaway" along the St. Lawrence River dates as early as 1825, when a young citizen of Montreal, John Young, suggested that an artificial "seaway" might be constructed along the St. Lawrence: one that would allow oceangoing ships to pass along the 2,300 miles from the Gulf of St. Lawrence to the westernmost point on Lake Superior. Postponement of the project between 1895 and the 1950s was due to the opposition of the seaway's construction by regional industries in both nations. Those who ran rail lines and citizens of existing ports along the Atlantic Ocean argued that an interior water route would take business away from them. Even coal companies were concerned that a vast seaway project would include the construction of hydroelectric power plants, causing a reduction in the amount of coal needed to produce electricity across the Northeast.

International politics also worked against the project. Because the portion of the St. Lawrence under question flowed along the borders of southern Quebec and Ontario and northern New York State, it was assumed that the project would have to be a cooperative, international effort. However, even in the late 1800s, the Canadian government still bore hard feelings over the opening of the Erie Canal in 1825. The canal had taken trade away from the St. Lawrence River, and many of the construction projects to improve water transportation on both sides of the United States–Canadian border had resulted in competition between the two North American trade powers.

In Canada, early projects such as the Welland Canal had been built as a direct answer to the challenge presented by New York's Erie Canal.

By the early 1930s, it appeared that the two nations were approaching an agreement. In July 1932, the U.S. Congress debated a proposal called the St. Lawrence Deep Waterway Treaty. The treaty called for the excavation of a 27-foot channel from Montreal to the Great Lakes. The construction project would also include the building of a large hydroelectric power facility; the power to be generated by rapids along the St. Lawrence. The electricity was to be shared by New York State and the province of Ontario.

Congress rejected the plan in 1934. Both the United States and Canada were locked in the depths of the Great Depression, and although a seaway project would generate thousands of jobs, there were questions concerning how such a vast construction program might be paid for. Again, railroads, Atlantic coast harbors, utility companies, and others were afraid that they would lose business to a giant seaway and its equally expansive power plant. Through the remainder of the 1930s, lobbyists in both countries kept the project from getting underway, despite the fact that leaders of both nations, including President Franklin Roosevelt, gave their political support to the seaway.

The plans for a St. Lawrence canal project languished until 1941, when President Roosevelt was urged by the project's supporters to resubmit the proposal to Congress. When the president did so, Congress appeared ready to give its support. Both nations entered an agreement to build the seaway and the power plant. Only a handful of legal questions remained to be answered before work could begin on the project. Before the year's end, however, the United States was pulled into World War II because of Japan's attack on Pearl Harbor in December. The seaway project was postponed again.

By the early 1950s, tired of delays, the Canadian government was preparing to pursue the construction of a seaway without help from the United States. A new U.S. president, Harry S. Truman, soon took up the cause of the seaway; he was determined to include the United States and fearful that the Canadians might build their own waterway. During the spring of 1952, Truman delivered letters to the members of the Senate and House of Representatives, urging members of congress to support the seaway:

> The question before the Congress now is not whether the seaway should be built, but whether the United States should share in its construction, operation, and control. The Canadian Government is ready and willing to build a deep seaway from Montreal to Lake Erie on the Canadian side of the boundary, if Congress does not authorize the United States government to participate in building the joint Canadian–United States Sea agreed to in 1941.[68]

Despite Truman's encouragement, Congress took no immediate action.

The Canadian government became frustrated and tired of waiting. The Canadian secretary of state for external affairs, Lester Pearson, expressed the frustration of many of Canada's seaway supporters: "The biggest and longest dragging of feet I have known in my entire career is that of the Americans on the St. Lawrence."[69] At the end of their collective patience, Canadian government officials began to make plans for a completely Canadian seaway project as early as 1951. As the Canadians prepared to begin work on the project, however, the U.S. Congress agreed to cooperate on construction of the long-proposed St. Lawrence Seaway. On May 13, 1954, the two governments signed the Wiley-Dondero Act, which recognized a joint agreement to finally build the North American inland sea lane.

On May 13, 1954, the U.S. Congress passed the Wiley-Dondero Act, agreeing to join Canada in the construction of the St. Lawrence Seaway. Construction (shown here) began in September of that year and the seaway officially opened on June 26, 1959.

BUILDING THE ST. LAWRENCE SEAWAY

The proposed seaway would prove to be a gigantic and complex excavation and building project even for two nations as resourceful as the United States and Canada:

> The St. Lawrence Seaway from Montreal to Lake Erie would include canals that were deepened to 27 feet. Construction workers would dig through dry land, as well as dredge the river bottom to make the route safe for most of the world's large ships. There would be a series of locks and dams that,

taken together, would lift ships about 600 feet above sea level as they moved 2,000 miles inland. In addition, a massive power plant along the river would provide energy to the seaway, as well as to parts of Canada and the United States. Construction of the seaway and its management would be the joint responsibility of the St. Lawrence Seaway Authority in Canada and the American St. Lawrence Seaway Development Corporation.[70]

The majority of the work on the seaway centered on a 200-mile leg of the St. Lawrence River between Montreal and an island group called Thousand Islands in the St. Lawrence at the outlet of Lake Ontario. More than half of this part of the St. Lawrence marked the border between the United States and Canada.

CLEARING THE WAY FOR CONSTRUCTION

Before work on the excavation of the route for the newly approved seaway could begin, the way had to be cleared. This included the removal of homes, businesses, and even whole towns. The building of the hydroelectric plant required the construction of a huge dam to supply a water reservoir. The dam created a 30-mile-long and 4-mile-wide lake, today called Lake St. Lawrence, and would allow ships using the seaway to bypass some of the wildest rapids on the river, the Long Sault Rapids. Eighteen thousand acres of land in New York and 20,000 acres in Ontario and Quebec were inundated, which required the removal of hundreds of residents. Lake waters swamped 600 homes and several hundred farms in New York and 200 Canadian farms. Seven Canadian towns, including Aultsville, Farran's Point, Dickinson's Landing, Wales, Milles Roches, Moulinette, and Iroquois, had to be evacuated.

The residents of Iroquois were the first to be evacuated, beginning in 1955. The Ontario Hydro Company made contact

with every resident and tried to assure them that they would
do everything possible to ease the residents' transition to their
new homes:

> They offered to construct new homes or buildings, or to
> move the old buildings onto new concrete foundations. . . .
> Existing homes were moved by two huge machines built
> in New Jersey at a cost of about $100,000 each. . . . After
> the houses had been moved, their owners' favorite shrubs
> followed. And if the owners wanted their homes placed next
> door to their old neighbors, that, too, was arranged. . . .
> While many people chose new homes, others chose to keep
> their old homes, which gave the newly transplanted commu-
> nities a more stable atmosphere. . . . All residents received
> new foundations, new plumbing, and new wiring for their
> homes, along with new streets, industrial parks, shopping
> centers, and schools. But for many people, new amenities
> could not replace the excitement of living along the river,
> watching the ships pass by, and feeling a part of the flow of
> the water.[71]

In all, 7,000 to 8,000 people were driven from their homes by
the St. Lawrence Seaway project. Most houses and businesses
only had to move a few miles from their original sites, but
the changes were upsetting and emotional for many. As they
prepared to make their move away from the river, the residents
of Iroquois tried to keep a positive attitude about the altera-
tions forced on their lives. For many, the town's new, unofficial
motto became "We have to go, but watch us grow!"[72]

CONSTRUCTION BEGINS

Once the local residents had been moved to safe ground, the
real work on the construction of the St. Lawrence Seaway
began. First, the river had to be drained or diverted from the

construction sites. This was a difficult job; it required the building of temporary cofferdams to rechannel the river. On the newly exposed "dry land," the excavation teams went to work cutting a deep channel for the seaway. As digging commenced, the excavation hit two different layers of geological formations. The first one was a sticky clay substance the workers called "blue goop." Below that lay a deep bed of ancient, ice-age rock "so hard that it stripped the teeth from power shovels after they had been digging only twelve hours."[73] Rock drills whose bits would normally last through 50 or 60 feet of rock drilling went blunt or cracked after only 5 feet.

Hard rock was a constant problem during excavation, and the winter weather along the Canada–New York border was also problematic. To stop construction during frigid winter months would have slowed the project needlessly, so work generally continued even in the bitter cold. The cold was hard on the workers, who struggled with harsh winds and frostbite: Their hands sometimes froze to tools. The weather was also harsh for equipment. Frozen metal tools snapped in half, and truckloads of earth and rock "had to be warmed before the loads could be dumped."[74] One major winter problem was how to pour concrete without it freezing while it set. The workers figured out a partial answer to this frustrating obstacle when they began to use glacial till, a natural mixture of gravel, sand, and clay. Glacial till would not freeze and crack despite the extreme cold.

Not only did workers have to excavate a new channel, they also had to build several locks for the new seaway. New locks near Montreal—the Côte St.-Catherine and St.-Lambert—were constructed to allow the river to pass the Lachine Rapids. Farther upriver from Montreal, the Upper and Lower Beauharnois Locks were constructed. These locks were capable of lifting a ship 84 feet up and down from Lake St. Francis. At Massena, New York, two additional locks, the Snell Lock and another named for President Dwight Eisenhower, were added.

The New York locks could raise ships up to the newly created Lake St. Lawrence. As ships moved beyond Lake St. Lawrence, they would need one more lock, the Iroquois Lock. This gave the seaway a total of seven locks, five in Canada and two on U.S. soil. Each lock was built large enough to accommodate ships as long as 730 feet and 75 feet in width, with a total ship and cargo tonnage of 29,000 tons. At the opening of the seaway in 1958, four out of five ships plying the waters of the world could use the seaway. The rest were too large. Workers also had to dredge the St. Lawrence to a uniform depth of 27 feet to ensure the passage of oceangoing cargo ships. Most of this effort was required on the U.S. leg of the river, especially the stretch running from Ogdensburg east to the Eisenhower Lock. On the U.S. side, workers constructed the Wiley-Dondero ship channel to bypass the power dam (it was later named the Moses-Saunders Dam) at Barnhart Island.

The work was done on a massive scale and required thousands of workers and giant pieces of equipment. Perhaps the largest of the excavation machines was one known by the workmen as "the Gentleman." This huge digging machine weighed 650 tons and had a shoveling capacity of 25 tons of rock, clay, and earth per bucket. When professionally operated, the machine could unearth and release a loaded, multiton scoop in less than a minute. In all, this machine and its smaller counterparts excavated more than 210 million cubic yards of earth in building the St. Lawrence Seaway. This amount of excavated material would fill a railroad of coal cars stretching east to west across the entire North American continent eight times over.

The work on the canal proved immense in scope: It was the "largest construction project ever carried out jointly by the United States and Canada."[75] At some points during the construction, as many as 22,000 people were employed to work on the seaway project. The work drew a steady stream of large crowds who came to witness the heavy machines and their progress along the St. Lawrence River. Everyone understood how important the project was and that every part of the construction had to be completed exactly according to the plans and specifications of the engineers who had developed the project. One mistake could have devastating results:

> Never before had such a powerful river been rearranged in such a major way. The thousands of homes and hundreds of towns that lined the banks would be in serious danger if a mistake caused the river to flood. An error in the water level of only 3 inches could spell disaster—too high, and villages would become islands; too low, and ships would be grounded.[76]

The workers and engineers on the St. Lawrence Seaway had to lower the river's depth, but they also had to raise the bridges above the river. The project called for new seaway specifications on bridges, requiring each to accommodate ships up to 120 feet tall. With some preexisting bridges, this specification was impossible and the bridge had to be replaced. Sometimes, the bridge could be modified and raised, as four bridges in the Montreal area were.

THE SEAWAY COMPLETED

By the summer of 1958, the St. Lawrence Seaway and all its support facilities, including the large power plant, were completed and ready for business. On July 1—Canada's national holiday, Dominion Day—planned explosions removed the cofferdam barriers that retained the waters of Lake St. Lawrence, and water began to pour into the seaway. Already, 100 ships were waiting, on both the St. Lawrence River and the Great Lakes, to take their turn passing through the locks. On the Fourth of July, the first ocean freighter passed through the seaway.

An aerial view of the St. Lawrence Seaway taken shortly after the waterway officially opened in 1959. The seaway is on the right side of the photo and both the Dwight D. Eisenhower and Bertrand H. Snell Locks, which are the only two locks operated by the United States, can be seen here.

A year later, the United States and Canada participated in dedication ceremonies attended by Queen Elizabeth II, whose royal yacht, *Britannia*, "sailed up the St. Lawrence, with U.S. President Dwight Eisenhower on board."[77] The prime minister of Canada was also in attendance at the special international ceremony, held on June 26, 1959. President Eisenhower spoke at the dedication and referred to the seaway's completion as "a tribute to those farsighted and persevering people who across the years pushed forward to their goal despite decades of disappointments and setbacks."[78] In her official address, the queen lauded the St. Lawrence Seaway as "a magnificent monument to the enduring friendship of our two nations."[79]

TAKING PASSAGE THROUGH THE ST. LAWRENCE SEAWAY

For nearly half a century, cargo ships from all over the world have arrived at the mouth of the St. Lawrence River assured of their ability to deliver their freight to any number of ports across the Great Lakes. The St. Lawrence Seaway, opened for business in 1958, continues to provide passage from the river to all five of the Great Lakes.

Modern ships must follow a rigorous ritual of passage from the Gulf of St. Lawrence through the Great Lakes. From the river's mouth to Montreal, ships proceed 1,000 miles upriver. Near Les Escoumins, just north of the confluence of the St. Lawrence and Saguenay Rivers, local professional pilots take the controls of commercial vessels and steer them through narrow channels and shallow waters.

Once a ship reaches Montreal, the ship owner must receive official permission to enter the St. Lawrence Seaway. There is a lane for all ships going upriver and another for those going downriver, which helps keep passing ships apart, avoiding accidents. Between Montreal and Lake Ontario, ships pass through seven locks. At each lock, light panels flash red, green, or yellow to indicate whether a lock is available (green), occupied (red), or how much time a ship must wait before preparing to enter a lock (several yellow lights indicate the delay time).

After passing through the first two locks (St.-Lambert and Côte Ste.-Catherine), ships proceed 16 miles to the next two, Lower and Upper Beauharnois Locks. Sixty miles farther upriver, ships pass through the Bertrand H. Snell and Dwight D. Eisenhower Locks, which are the only two operated by the United States. After almost 200 miles more, cargo vessels reach the Iroquois Lock. For the next 80 miles—to Lake Ontario—ships pass along the scenic Thousand Islands.

The vessels that continue to Lake Erie pass across 180 miles of Lake Ontario to the Welland Ship Canal, located west of Niagara Falls, where the canal's eight locks raise ships more than 300 feet—the longest lift of the entire canal complex—to the waters of Lake Erie. The Welland Locks are "twinned," allowing traffic to pass both upriver and down simultaneously.

Although most of the traffic that passes through the St. Lawrence Seaway consists of larger cargo vessels, both lakers and smaller, ocean-going vessels can also use the seaway. Specifications require such craft to measure at least 20 feet in length and weigh close to one ton. If such a small boat, most of which are pleasure craft, arrives at a lock at the same time as a cargo vessel, the cargo vessel is always given first use.

8

Epilogue

Nearly half a century after its lock and passage system opened for business, the St. Lawrence Seaway remains a busy inland thoroughfare for oceangoing commerce. The seaway is a major economic entity in the region of the St. Lawrence and the Great Lakes, creating nearly 45,000 jobs in the United States alone; these jobs produce $2 billion in personal income annually. Many of these jobs are directly related to the work done onboard ships or by dock and port workers; other workers include truckers who haul freight to and from the seaway's ports. An equal amount of income is generated by Canadian workers connected to the St. Lawrence Seaway.

Throughout the passage of nearly five decades, the amount of freight transported through the canal has remained considerable, adding to the level of trade in many inland ports, many of which today handle 20 to 100 times more freight and cargo than they did prior to the seaway's opening. The most common commodity shipped through the canal is wheat, with 12 million tons transported in 1991. Iron ore is the second most important commodity by weight. Since the seaway opened in 1958, more than one billion tons of cargo, with an estimated worth greater than $200 billion, has passed east and west along the seaway.

Prior to the construction of the seaway, inland railroad companies opposed the system, claiming that it would provide considerable competition to its services. This fear has proven true. Shipping produce, raw materials, and finished industrial products on the seaway is cheaper per ton per mile than shipping these same commodities by railroad. The transportation costs for delivering goods bound for a foreign port by rail from Chicago, Illinois, to a seaport on the Atlantic are greater than using the seaway. In pure economic terms, the seaway remains a bargain in the world of transportation. The seaway does not compete with railroads year-round, however. Every year, the St. Lawrence Seaway is closed for approximately three months during the winter because of ice. In a typical year, the seaway closes during the final two weeks of December and remains free of cargo ships until late March or early April:

> Because of ice, the St. Lawrence Seaway and the Great Lakes are only navigable for nine months a year. Some locks along the seaway use giant air pumps to churn up the cold water and keep it from freezing solid. It is too expensive to keep all the canals and locks on the entire seaway free of ice throughout the winter, however. The last ships must get through the seaway before the end of the year or risk being stuck in ice until spring. Montreal, however, is the most important port in eastern Canada. Icebreakers—tough ships designed to smash through ice—keep the port's channels clear all year-round, so cargo ships can reach the city from the ocean.[80]

Some of the early problems the seaway experienced have been solved over the years. When the St. Lawrence Seaway opened, ships were able to pass through the main section of the seaway's new lock system without much delay. Ships passing to and from the St. Lawrence and Lake Ontario, however, were held up by the Welland Canal, creating water-bound traffic jams. Because the Welland system is much older than the St. Lawrence Seaway, it moves ships less quickly, frequently causing ships to wait their turn to pass. During the early 1970s, the Welland system was augmented and modernized by a new eight-mile channel section, allowing seaway traffic to bypass Welland, Ontario, and eliminating the bottleneck in the St. Lawrence canal system.

Other problems persist. The seaway has been used to haul incredible amounts of freight, but the system has never technically managed a profit. The St. Lawrence Seaway proved so costly to construct that, even though the ships that use the seaway pay tolls with each passage, the cost of construction has never been fully recouped. Early seaway proponents promised

The St. Lawrence Seaway usually closes for the winter during the last couple of weeks of December and remains closed until the ice thins in late March or early April. Here, a Canadian ship makes its way through the Eisenhower Lock, near Messina, New York, in early April.

that the expensive system would generate profits and the system's tolls would cover the costs of construction. This promise has proven difficult to achieve. Over the decades, the Canadian government has been forced to raise the toll rates it charges on the seaway to help cover costs and debt. Hopeful seaway officials promised that the St. Lawrence Seaway would reach its full capacity of use by the early 1990s. That prediction did not come to fruition. Despite its constant use, the seaway has remained a canal system operating at less than full capacity:

In it first years of operation, the seaway transported about 30 million tons of cargo each year. This amount increased steadily, reaching a peak of 74 million tons in 1979. Since then, however, the transportation of cargo has declined. Today, the seaway transports less than 45 million tons per year, or approximately seven percent of the world's total. This is only half of what the seaway system could potentially carry.[81]

One of the seaway's problems is its age. Since its opening in 1958, ship dimensions have increased dramatically. Today, only one out of eight of the world's merchant vessels, as well as 5 percent of the container fleet, can fit into the St. Lawrence Seaway's locks and channels. In addition, the seaway's infrastructure is currently "in need of a major refit, with current maintenance requirements necessitating a winter shutdown and increasing repair costs as time goes by."[82] In 2003, the U.S. Army Corps of Engineers (USACE) completed a significant report that included suggestions for future refitting and expansion of the seaway. The USACE's research suggested that the seaway could provide additional economic development to North American shipping in the immediate future. Still, upgrades, improvements, and other significant changes will have to be made to the system—soon.

Despite its limitations, however, the seaway has made and continues to make significant economic contributions to the river valley and lake system it has served since the late 1950s. Just as the St. Lawrence River provided the impetus for the establishment of colonial outposts such as Quebec City and Montreal, the modern river and its seaway continue to contribute significantly to their economy and growth. Today, Quebec City is a major industrial urban center of Canada, famous for its textile mills, pulp and paper mills, and chemical plants. Similarly, Montreal is Canada's second-largest port, profiting from \$300 million in commodity shipping alone. Its industrial landscape includes meat-packing plants, clothing and pharmaceutical facilities, and oil refineries.

Quebec and Montreal are only two of the Canadian ports that have reaped the advantages of the St. Lawrence Seaway; others include Hamilton and Toronto, Ontario, two ports on Lake Ontario. These two Great Lakes cities boast steel and chemical facilities, as well as meat-packing and furniture plants. In the United States, the five leading ports that rely on trade goods passing through the St. Lawrence corridor are Buffalo, New York; Chicago, Illinois; Detroit, Michigan; Milwaukee, Wisconsin; and Cleveland, Ohio.

The St. Lawrence River region was first tapped by Europeans for its riches in fur, but the development of other commodities has helped nurture the industrial base found along the modern St. Lawrence Valley. Near the river's mouth, in Labrador—the barren, rocky land Cartier called "land of Cain"—immense deposits of iron ore were discovered during the mid-twentieth century, spawning a mining industry in a region formerly known primarily for its fishing industry. Today, St. Lawrence port towns such as Tadoussac and Sept-Îles, ship out not only iron ore, but also other metal ores, including aluminum and titanium. In the former New France whaling town of Tadoussac stands one of the largest aluminum plants in the world. The longtime fishing village of Sept-Îles ships out great quantities of iron ore, making it Canada's third-largest port. The port of Trois-Rivières today is the "Newsprint Capital of the World": Each year, 100 million logs are routed to the former New France fort. This vast sea of wood is processed into hundreds of thousands of tons of newsprint; the paper used in the printing of newspapers.

With the development of modern industry and the mushrooming of urban populations along the St. Lawrence River and Seaway, pollution has become a significant regional concern. Ecologists have targeted pollution as the greatest threat to the St. Lawrence at the beginning of the twenty-first century:

> The river's greatest challenge today is environmental. Canadian and American scientists have identified mercury, PCBs, and other heavy metal contaminants stored in the flesh of game fish. Layered in the sediment in many locations and downstream of many cities, this contamination is not going away quickly and would be impossible to remove. Despite talking a good game of environmental concern on a global scale, Canada has not been the best of stewards along its greatest river.[83]

During the 1980s and 1990s, environmental improvement efforts targeted the ecological challenges the river faces. In 1988, the Canadian government announced its St. Lawrence Action Plan, which established specific goals for conserving the waters and the general environment of the St. Lawrence. Among its proposals were a 90 percent reduction in liquid toxic waste being dumped into the Canadian river system by 50 industrial plants, as well as wetlands restoration, and the development of a marine park at the mouth of the Saguenay River to protect area wildlife. In the United States, Congress passed the United States Oil Pollution Act of 1990, which required all oil tankers to be double hulled. The program called for the removal of all single-hulled tankers in 1995, and the changeover is ongoing. The Great Lakes/St. Lawrence Pollution Prevention Initiative, a joint U.S.-Canadian program, was launched in 1991. Armed with an initial $25 million, the program is "dedicated to involving all of society in reducing toxic pollutants."[84] Other environmental groups in Canada have created a pollution awareness system called the Zones of Prime Concern. Twenty-three such "zones" have been pinpointed along the course of the St. Lawrence River. (For additional information on Canada's St. Lawrence River conservation project, enter "St. Lawrence Action Plan" into any search engine and browse the many sites listed.)

Even with its current levels of pollution and contamination, the St. Lawrence continues to serve the people and economies of eastern Canada and the United States as a vital waterway. The river is a natural flight corridor for game birds, such as Canadian geese, and provides a natural habitat for many birds. Nearly a quarter-million snow geese pass through Cap Tourmente annually. Other birds—including blue herons, pintail ducks, killdeer, loons, and kingfishers—still nest in the wetlands of the St. Lawrence system. These wetlands are invaluable to wildlife, providing habitats for more than 220 species of birds, mammals, and aquatic marine life. Fish are still abundant in the river's waters, and sportsmen flock to the St. Lawrence and its tributaries in search of speckled trout, bass, and northern pike, and ducks such as goldeneyes and buffleheads. Sports fishing remains a huge business for the St. Lawrence region: Annual revenues are estimated at $4 billion. The numbers of some species, including muskies and sturgeon, have declined during the past several decades because of overfishing and commercial exploitation. Pollution also has had damaging effects on several species of fish in the St. Lawrence and the Great Lakes:

> Of the ten most highly valued species of fish in Lake Ontario, seven have almost completely disappeared. In fact, toxic substances in the Great Lakes have had damaging effects on all fish populations. Salmon, trout, and whitefish do not reach full sexual development, and coho salmon and lake trout show enlarged thyroid glands. Big sores show up on the bodies of other fish that were once healthy and plentiful in the St. Lawrence River. Some are deformed, and many have an unusual reddish cast to their gills.[85]

THE LURE OF THOUSAND ISLANDS

Native Americans knew them as Manatoana, the "Garden of the Great Spirit." Today, the nearly 2,000 islands that dot the mouth of the origins of the St. Lawrence River are known as the Thousand Islands. These tree-covered islands are part of one of the most scenic portions of the great North American river and a popular international tourism destination, which includes towns and communities along both sides of the U.S.-Canadian border.

Although geologists explain the islands strictly in scientific terms as the peaks of smaller hills that have protruded above the waters of the river, ancient Indian peoples created an infinitely more romantic tale of origin. According to the legend, the Great Spirit was so concerned about the constant warfare taking place among rival tribes that he created a garden paradise where all Indians could live in peace and harmony with one another. The Great Spirit's newly created paradise did not stop his people from fighting one another, however. Disappointed, the Great Spirit gathered up his paradise in an immense blanket and prepared to fly it back to his heavenly residence. While in flight, the Spirit's blanket ripped open and his paradise of peace fell toward the St. Lawrence River, where it crashed and broke into a thousand bits of land, each becoming an island.

The islands stretch along the river for 50 miles, from Cape Vincent to Ogdensburg, New York. Tourists come to the islands and their resort environment largely for the great fishing, as well as the peace and quiet,

The ecology of the St. Lawrence and the Great Lakes has also been disturbed by the introduction of new species, delivered to North America as hitchhikers on the hulls of ships from around the world. Nonnative invaders, such as Zebra mussels, which arrived in the ballast water of oceangoing vessels, now menace the river and lakes, clogging up intake pipes on water treatment plants, city water systems, hydroelectric cooling stations, and even recreational boat motors. Loosestrife, a European plant variety, has also reached the St. Lawrence, where it chokes out native vegetation, a source of food for domestic fish and animal life.

taking refuge in dozens of local hotels and bed and breakfasts. One of the many resort communities located in the Thousand Islands, the small town of Clayton was home to Sophia LaLonde, who probably did more to put Thousand Islands on the map than any other person. During the early 1900s, LaLonde's husband, George, worked as a fishing tour guide on the St. Lawrence. After a day's fishing, Mr. LaLonde would provide his guests with a shoreside dinner, where they were introduced to a special salad dressing his wife had created—a mixture of mayonnaise, ketchup, and pickle relish. The dressing was always a big hit with visiting tourists. One of them, May Irwin, a well-known New York actress, asked Sophia for the recipe, which she then gave to George C. Boldt, the owner of the prestigious Waldorf-Astoria Hotel. (Ms. Irwin had also been served the special dressing at the Herald Hotel, where she had stayed while visiting Thousand Islands. Sophia had given the recipe to the hotel's owner, Mrs. Ella Bertrand.) Boldt enjoyed the dressing so much that he ordered his chef to add it to the hotel's dining room menu. Soon, the dressing was a popular favorite. It was Ms. Irwin who named the dressing she had discovered on vacation— Thousand Island dressing.

In 1972, Clayton was still home to the descendents of Sophia and George LaLonde. The town's Herald Hotel still stands and was renamed in 1972 the Thousand Islands Inn. The inn sells 5,000 bottles of its "Original Recipe" dressing annually.

Today, the St. Lawrence River remains singular in its importance to the region it has crossed for thousands of years. As with many modern rivers, for those who live along its banks or use its waters for drinking, hunting, fishing, recreation, and industrial purposes or as a trade corridor to and from a wider world, the twenty-first century must become one in which the balance between commerce and conservation, population and preservation, and man and nature must be maintained or, in some cases, restored.

13,000–10,000 B.P.   Region of the modern-day St. Lawrence River valley is covered with a massive buildup of ice more than a mile thick; the glacial shifts help create the river's valley.

5,000–3,000 B.P.   Early humans settle the St. Lawrence River region.

A.D. 1000–1500   Native Americans develop their modern-day tribal systems, which are in place by the time the first Europeans arrive.

1497   Genoese sea captain Giovanni Caboto (John Cabot) sails to New World and reaches Newfoundland, near the mouth of the St. Lawrence.

1524   First French-sponsored voyage to North America, under the command of Giovanni da Verrazzano, reaches Newfoundland.

1534   Huron Indians along the St. Lawrence meet with

5,000–3,000 B.P.
First Native Americans arrive in St. Lawrence region

1535
Cartier names Gulf of St. Lawrence "La Baye Sainct Laurins"

1534
Jacques Cartier meets Huron Indians along the St. Lawrence

1608
Samuel de Champlain founds Quebec

1680s–1690s
Work on Lachine Canal begins but abandoned in 1701

5,000–3,000 B.P.   A.D. 1000–1500   1800

A.D. 1000–1500
Native Americans in St. Lawrence region develop modern-day tribal systems

1497
John Cabot reaches Newfoundland, near the mouth of the St. Lawrence

1763
British take over St. Lawrence Valley after French and Indian War

1791
Canada divided into Upper Canada (Ontario) and Lower Canada (Quebec) by Great Britain

French explorer Jacques Cartier after he reaches the St. Lawrence River.

1535 During second voyage to modern-day Canada, Cartier gives the Gulf of St. Lawrence its modern name: "La Baye Sainct Laurins"; on reaching the Indian village of Hochelaga, he names the site "Mont Real."

1543 French colonizer Jean-François de la Rocque, sieur de Roberval, fails in his attempt to establish a permanent French colony along the St. Lawrence River.

Late 1500s French merchants sail up the St. Lawrence River and begin to trade for furs at the Indian trading site of Tadoussac, near the Saguenay River, a tributary of the St. Lawrence.

1600s–1700s Native American alliance, the Abenaki Confederacy, is

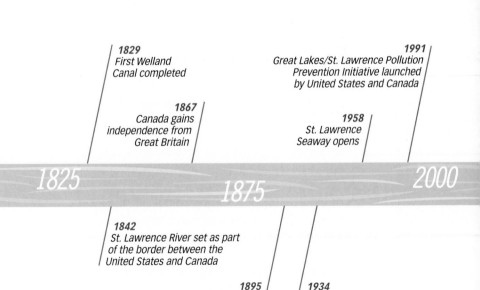

1829
First Welland
Canal completed

1991
Great Lakes/St. Lawrence Pollution
Prevention Initiative launched
by United States and Canada

1867
Canada gains
independence from
Great Britain

1958
St. Lawrence
Seaway opens

1825   1875   2000

1842
St. Lawrence River set as part
of the border between the
United States and Canada

1895
United States and Canada
discuss building
St. Lawrence Seaway

1934
United States calls for joint
U.S.-Canadian construction
of St. Lawrence Seaway

established among St. Lawrence tribes; it includes the Western and Eastern Abenaki, Malecite, Passamaquoddy, and Micmac.

1603–1605 French explorer and colonizer Samuel de Champlain explores Nova Scotia and scouts along the North American coast for a colony site.

1607 French establish permanent settlement at Port Royal, on the coast of Nova Scotia.

1608 Champlain founds the French colony of Quebec.

1629 Champlain surrenders Quebec to an English fleet; English hold Quebec for the next three years.

1620s AND 1630s Champlain continues to support his colony along the St. Lawrence, earning himself the name "father of New France"; he dies in 1635.

1642 French nobleman and military veteran Paul de Chomedey, sieur de Maisonneuve, establishes a Jesuit missionary town at Mont Real.

1670 Jesuit Father François de Salignac of Montreal proposes the excavation of a canal between Montreal and Lachine to bypass Lachine Rapids; the canal is not built.

1680s–1690s Under the direction of Father François Dollier de Casson, work is begun on Lachine Canal, but the project is abandoned in 1701.

1689 Iroquois warriors attack French village of Lachine, located upriver from Montreal, killing 60 people.

1690s Fighting between the English and French along the St. Lawrence Valley includes English raids on Port Royal, La Prairie, and Vercheres (King William's War, 1689–1697).

1702–1713 Queen Anne's War. During the fighting along the St. Lawrence, New Englanders capture Port Royal but fail to capture Quebec.

1713 French erect a new fortress to protect Quebec from future English raids.

1740–1747 King George's War. French fortress at Louisbourg, which protected the mouth of the St. Lawrence, is captured by New Englanders in 1745; English fail in plans to capture Montreal and Quebec; Treaty of Aix-la-Chapelle (1748) restores Louisbourg to the French.

1754–1763 French and Indian War: British capture Louisbourg in 1758, Quebec in 1759, and Montreal in 1760, effectively ending French control of Canada.

1763 French expelled from North America under Treaty of Paris; St. Lawrence Valley falls under British domination.

1775–1776 Two-pronged American invasion of Canada during first year of the American Revolution fails to capture Quebec.

1780–1800 A half-million new residents settle along the St. Lawrence River.

1791 British government of Canada divides British Canada into Upper Canada (Ontario) and Lower Canada (Quebec).

1825 Lachine Canal is completed to provide competition for American Erie Canal; that same year, Montreal citizen John Young suggests an artificial "seaway" to connect the St. Lawrence to the westernmost point on Lake Superior.

1829 First Welland Canal, designed to bypass ships around Niagara Falls, is completed.

1830 Immigrants arrive in British Canada, passing through Quebec, at the rate of 30,000 annually.

1842 Webster-Ashburton Treaty sets the St. Lawrence River as part of the border between the United States and Canada.

1842–1845 Changes and improvements are made to the Welland Canal, including the enlargement of its locks to a width of 25 feet and a reduction in the number of locks from 40 to 27.

1843–1848 Lachine Canal is enlarged to accommodate larger ships.

1867 Canada gains independence from Great Britain and establishes the Confederation of the Dominion of Canada.

1873–1884 Lachine Canal is again enlarged.

1886 Mohawk Indian ironworkers are employed by the Canadian Pacific Railroad to build a bridge across the St. Lawrence River near Montreal.

1887 Welland Canal is augmented to take a more direct route from Port Dalhousie to Allanburg, abandoning the Twelve Mile Creek leg of the former canal.

1895 Discussions held between representatives of the United States and Canada concerning possible construction of St. Lawrence Seaway; talks fail to lead to action.

1907 While under construction, the Quebec Bridge collapses into the St. Lawrence, killing nearly 100 workmen, including 33 Mohawks.

1929 By this year, 15,000 ships were passing through the Lachine Canal's locks annually.

1934 U.S. Congress rejects St. Lawrence Deep Waterway Treaty, calling for joint U.S.-Canadian construction of St. Lawrence Seaway.

1954 United States and Canada sign Wiley-Dondero Act, a joint agreement to finally build the North American inland sea lane.

1958 St. Lawrence Seaway, a joint canal project of the United States and Canada, is opened for business, facilitating oceangoing traffic from the Atlantic to the Great Lakes.

1959 Official dedication of the opening of the St. Lawrence Seaway includes Queen Elizabeth II and President Dwight D. Eisenhower.

1970s Welland Canal system is augmented and modernized by a new eight-mile channel section.

1988 Canadian government announces St. Lawrence Action Plan, to establish specific goals for conserving waters and environment of the St. Lawrence River.

1991 Joint U.S.-Canadian program, the Great Lakes/ St. Lawrence Pollution Prevention Initiative is launched; it is "dedicated to involving all of society in reducing toxic pollutants" on both water systems.

2003 U.S. Army Corps of Engineers completes report that suggests future refitting and expansion of St. Lawrence Seaway.

NOTES

CHAPTER 1:
The River That Walks

1 Trudy J. Hanmer, *The St. Lawrence* (New York: Franklin Watts, 1984), 6.

2 Ibid.

3 Ibid., 8.

CHAPTER 2:
Natives along the River

4 Tim McNeese, ed., *Myths of Native America* (New York: Four Walls Eight Windows, 2003), 10.

5 Barry M. Pritzker, *A Native American Encyclopedia: History, Culture, and Peoples* (New York: Oxford University Press, 2000), 508.

6 Ibid., 413.

CHAPTER 3:
The French Reach the St. Lawrence

7 Thomas B. Costain, *The White and the Gold: The French Regime in Canada* (Garden City, N.Y.: Doubleday & Company, 1954), 4.

8 Ibid., 17.

9 Peter Charles Hoffer, *The Brave New World: A History of Early America* (Boston, Mass.: Houghton Mifflin, 2000).

10 Costain, *The White and the Gold*, 20.

11 Ibid., 19–20.

12 Ibid., 20.

13 Ibid.

14 George M. Wrong, *The Rise and Fall of New France*, vol. 1 (New York: Octagon Books, 1970), 54.

15 *The European Challenge* (Alexandria, Va.: Time-Life Books, 1992), 66.

16 Samuel Eliot Morison, *Samuel de Champlain: Father of New France* (Boston, Mass.: Little, Brown and Company, 1972), 5–6.

17 Costain, *The White and the Gold*, 27.

18 Ibid., 33.

19 Ibid., 39.

20 Ibid., 45.

21 Morison, *Samuel de Champlain: Father of New France*, 11.

CHAPTER 4:
The Father of New France

22 *The European Challenge*, 71.

23 Costain, *The White and the Gold*, 52–53.

24 Hoffer, *The Brave New World: A History of Early America*, 132.

25 Morison, *Samuel de Champlain: Father of New France*, 63.

26 Ibid., 68.

27 Costain, *The White and the Gold*, 63.

28 *The European Challenge*, 72.

29 Costain, *The White and the Gold*, 65.

30 Ibid.

31 Ibid., 66.

32 Ibid., 67.

33 Ibid., 68.

34 Ibid., 69.

35 *The European Challenge*, 72.

36 Morison, *Samuel de Champlain: Father of New France*, 111.

37 Costain, *The White and the Gold*, 72.

38 Ibid., 75.

39 Ibid.

40 Ibid., 84.

41 Ibid., 89.

42 Morison, *Samuel de Champlain: Father of New France*, 213–214.

43 Costain, *The White and the Gold*, 122.

44 Morison, *Samuel de Champlain: Father of New France*, 218.

45 Ibid., 224.

46 Ibid., 226.

47 Ibid., 217.

CHAPTER 5:
War along the River

48 George M. Wrong, *The Rise and Fall of New Fance*, vol. 2 (New York: Octagon Books, 1970), 506.

49 Hoffer, *The Brave New World: A History of Early America*, 297.

50 Wrong, *The Rise and Fall of New Fance,* vol. 2, 679.

51 Hoffer, *The Brave New World: A History of Early America,* 437.

52 Ibid., 440.

53 Ibid., 444.

54 Ibid.

55 Ibid., 446.

56 Wrong, *The Rise and Fall of New Fance,* vol. 2, 846–847.

57 Ibid., 848–849.

58 Bruce Lancaster, *History of the American Revolution* (New York: Simon and Schuster, 2003), 125.

59 Ibid., 122.

60 David Hawke, *The Colonial Experience* (Indianapolis, Ind.: Bobbs-Merrill, 1966), 602.

61 Lancaster, *History of the American Revolution,* 124.

62 Hawke, *The Colonial Experience,* 602.

63 Ibid., 603.

64 Hanmer, *The St. Lawrence,* 26.

CHAPTER 6:
Recreating the River

65 Terri Willis, *St. Lawrence: River and Seaway* (Austin, Tex.: Raintree Steck-Vaughn, 1995), 22.

66 Ibid.

67 Hanmer, *The St. Lawrence,* 29.

CHAPTER 7:
The St. Lawrence Seaway

68 Willis, *St. Lawrence: River and Seaway,* 26.

69 Ibid., 27.

70 Ibid., 29.

71 Ibid., 32.

72 Ibid., 31.

73 Hanmer, *The St. Lawrence,* 35.

74 Ibid.

75 Willis, *St. Lawrence: River and Seaway,* 33.

76 Ibid., 34.

77 Ibid., 40.

78 Ibid.

79 Ibid.

CHAPTER 8:
Epilogue

80 Tim Cooke, *The St. Lawrence River* (Milwaukee, Wisc.: Gareth Stevens Publishing, 2004), 25.

81 Willis, *St. Lawrence: River and Seaway,* 52.

82 *www.grandslacs-voiemaritime.com/ en/aboutus/system_review.html.*

83 *http://www.vsa.cape.com/~powens/ riverhistory.htm.*

84 Willis, *St. Lawrence: River and Seaway,* 56.

85 Ibid.

Athearn, Robert G. *American Heritage Illustrated History of the United States. Vol. 1: The New World.* New York: Choice, Inc., 1988.

———. *American Heritage Illustrated History of the United States. Vol. 2: Colonial America.* New York: Choice, Inc., 1988.

———. *American Heritage Illustrated History of the United States. Vol. 3: The Revolution.* New York: Choice, Inc., 1988.

Beckett, Harry. *Waterways to the Great Lakes.* Vero Beach, Fla.: The Rourke Corporation, Inc., 1999.

Blue, Rose, and Corinne J. Naden. *Exploring the St. Lawrence River Region.* Chicago, Ill.: Raintree, 2004.

Bonvillain, Nancy. *The Huron.* New York: Chelsea House, 1989.

Charbonneau, Hubert, Bertrand Desjardins, and Andre Guillemette. *The First French Canadians: Pioneers of the St. Lawrence Valley.* Newark, Del.: University of Delaware Press, 1993.

Cooke, Tim. *The St. Lawrence River.* Milwaukee, Wisc.: Gareth Stevens Publishing, 2004.

Costain, Thomas B. *The White and the Gold: The French Regime in Canada.* Garden City, N.Y.: Doubleday, 1954.

Dillon, Richard H. *North American Indian Wars.* New York: Facts on File, 1983.

The European Challenge. Alexandria, Va.: Time-Life Books, 1992.

Fischer, George, and Claude Bouchard. *Sentinels in the Stream: Lighthouses of the St. Lawrence River.* Erin, Ont.: Boston Mills, 2001.

Hanmer, Trudy J. *The St. Lawrence.* New York: Franklin Watts, 1984.

Hawke, David. *The Colonial Experience.* Indianapolis, Ind.: The Bobbs-Merrill Company, 1966.

Hoffer, Peter Charles. *The Brave New World: A History of Early America.* Boston, Mass.: Houghton Mifflin, 2000.

Josephy, Alvin, Jr. *500 Nations: An Illustrated History of North American Indians.* New York: Alfred A. Knopf, 1994.

———. *The Indian Heritage of America.* Boston, Mass.: Houghton Mifflin, 1991.

Lancaster, Bruce. *History of the American Revolution.* New York: Simon and Schuster, 2003.

MacDonald, Robert. *The Owners of Eden: The Life and Past of the Native People* (Canada II). Calgary, Alberta: The Ballantrae Foundation, 1974.

———. *The Uncharted Nations: A Reference History of the Canadian Tribes* (Canada III). Calgary, Alberta: The Ballantrae Foundation, 1978.

———. *Years & Years Ago: A Prehistory* (Canada I). Calgary, Alberta: The Ballantrae Foundation, 1971.

Mackey, Frank. *Steamboat Connections: Montreal to Upper Canada, 1816–1843.* Montreal, Que.: McGill-Queen's University Press, 2000.

Malcolm, Andrew H. *The Canadians.* New York: Times Books, 1985.

Marteau, Robert. *River without End: A Logbook of the Saint Lawrence.* Toronto, Ont.: Exile Editions, 1987.

McNeese, Tim, ed. *Myths of Native America.* New York: Four Walls Eight Windows, 2003.

Morison, Samuel Eliot. *Samuel de Champlain: Father of New France.* Boston, Mass.: Little, Brown and Company, 1972.

Page, Jake. *In the Hands of the Great Spirit: The 20,000-Year History of American Indians.* New York: Free Press, 2003.

Pritzker, Barry M. *A Native American Encyclopedia: History, Culture, and Peoples.* New York: Oxford University Press, 2000.

Realm of the Iroquois. Alexandria, Va.: Time-Life Books, 1993.

Sagon-King, Alfred F., and E.B. "Skip" Gillham. *The Changing Seaway.* St. Catharines, Ont.: 1985.

Shaw, David W. *Inland Passage: On Boats & Boating in the Northeast.* New Brunswick, N.J.: Rutgers University Press, 1998.

Tebbel, John, ed. *The Battle for North America: From the Works of Francis Parkman.* Garden City, N.Y.: Doubleday, 1948.

Willis, Terri. *St. Lawrence: River and Seaway.* Austin, Tex.: Raintree Steck-Vaughn, 1995.

Winks, Honor Leigh, and Robin W. Winks. *The St. Lawrence.* East Sussex, U.K.: Hodder Wayland, 1980.

Wrong, George M. *The Rise and Fall of New France.* Vol. 1–2. New York: Octagon, 1970.

Beacock Fryer, Mary. *Pictorial History of the Thousand Islands of the St. Lawrence River*. Brockville, Ont.: Besancourt, 1977.

Fischer, George. *Sentinels in the Stream: Lighthouses of the St. Lawrence River*. Boston, Mass.: Mills Press, 2001.

———. *Castles and Cottages: River Retreats of the Thousand Islands*. Boston, Mass.: Mills Press, 2004.

Hamel, Jean-Francois. *The St. Lawrence: The Untamed Beauty of the Great River*. Montreal, Que.: Editions de L'Homme, 2004.

Jenkins, Phil. *River Song: Sailing the History of the St. Lawrence*. New York: Penguin, 2001.

Mackey, Frank. *Steamboat Connections: Montreal to Upper Canada, 1816–1843*. Montreal, Que.: McGill-Queen's University Press, 2003.

The St. Lawrence Center. *The St. Lawrence Ecosystem*. Sainte-Foy, Que.: Editions MultiMondes, 1996.

WEBSITES

St. Lawrence River Information
http://www.aquatic.uoguelph.ca/rivers/stlawr.htm

Great Lakes St. Lawrence Seaway System
http://www.grandslacs-voiemaritime.com/

St. Lawrence River and Seaway Information
http://www.great-lakes.net/lakes/stlaw.html

Quebec Tourist Guide to the St. Lawrence River
http://www.quebecweb.com/tourisme/fleuveang.html

St. Lawrence County, New York
http://www.st-lawrence.ny.us/

St. Lawrence River History
http://www.vsa.cape.com/~powens/riverhistory.htm

ABOUT THE AUTHOR

TIM McNEESE is an Associate Professor of History at York College in York, Nebraska, where he is currently in his thirteenth year of instruction. Professor McNeese earned an Associate of Arts degree from York College, a Bachelor of Arts in history and political science from Harding University, and a Master of Arts in history from Southwest Missouri State University.

A prolific author of books for elementary, middle and high school, and college readers, McNeese has published more than 70 books and educational materials over the past 20 years, on everything from Indian mythology to the building of the Great Wall of China. His writing has earned him a citation in the library reference work, *Something about the Author*. His wife, Beverly, is an Assistant Professor of English at York College and the couple has two children, Noah and Summer. Readers are encouraged to contact Professor McNeese at tdmcneese@york.edu.